Choosing the Right Regulatory Career

Edited by Peggy Berry, MBA, RAC

Copyright © 2010 by the Regulatory Affairs Professionals Society.

All rights reserved.

ISBN: 978-0-9787006-7-6

At the time of publication, all Internet references (URLs) in this book were valid. However, these references are subject to change without notice.

Book Design by Karol A. Keane, Keanedesign.org

Making better healthcare products possible℠

5635 Fishers Lane
Suite 550
Rockville, MD 20852
USA

Tel +1 301 770 2920
Fax +1 301 770 2924

Washington, DC ▪ Brussels ▪ Tokyo

RAPS.org

Contributing Authors

Regulatory careers cover a range of activities, products and environments, and it is this variety that makes the field so interesting and so challenging. My thanks to the authors who have shared their stories in this book to help others find their own niche in the regulatory profession.

Peggy Berry, MBA, RAC
VP/Head of Quality & Regulatory Affair, Amarin Pharma Inc.
Editor and Primary Author

Contributing Authors

Stephanie Anderson
Student, Humber Institute of Information and Technology's Regulatory Affairs program

Linda Bowen, MS, RAC
Regulatory Intelligence US Region
Sanofi-Aventis

Meredith Brown-Tuttle, RAC
Regulatory Consultant
TekTeam

Kimberly Carneal
Senior Manager, Regulatory and Government Affairs
BioMarin Pharmaceutical Inc.

Christine Conroy
VP, Regulatory Affairs and GCP Compliance
Affymax

Kathryn Davidson, RAC
Director, Regulatory Operations
BioMarin Pharmaceutical Inc.

Katie Ditton, RAC
Senior Manager, Regulatory Operations
BioMarin Pharmaceutical Inc.

Anne-Virginie Eggimann, MSc
General Manager
Voisin Consulting Inc.

Mary Lou Freathy, JD
Vice President, Quality & Regulatory Affairs
Paddock Laboratories

Paul Gil, PhD, RAC
Deputy Director of Global Regulatory Affairs
Bayer Healthcare

Bonnie J. Goldmann, MD
Independent Consultant
Goldmann Consulting LLC

Amy Grant
Director of Regulatory Strategy and Science
ViroPharma Inc.

Joseph Greer, RAC
Senior Director, QA, CMC & DEA Compliance
Paddock Laboratories

Nancy R. Katz, PhD
President and Principal Medical Writing Consultant
Illyria Consulting Group Inc.

Evangeline D. Loh, PhD, RAC
Vice President of Regulatory Affairs
Emergo

Robert Myers, PhD
Independent Consultant
RAM Pharma

Scott Oglesby, PhD
Director, Executive Consulting
Beckloff Associates

Nancy Pire Smerkanich
Vice President, Global Regulatory Affairs
Octagon Research Solutions Inc.

Helene Sou, MSc, RAC
Project Leader
Voisin Consulting Inc.

Theresa M. Straut, CIP, RAC
Director
Independent IRB

Table of Contents

1. Introduction 1
   By Peggy Berry, MBA, RAC
2. Support Groups and Organizations for Regulatory Professionals 7
   By Amy Grant
3. Education 13
   By Kathryn Davidson, RAC
4. Human Dynamics of Regulatory 25
   By Amy Grant
5. Working as an Independent Regulatory Consultant 31
   By Helene Sou, MSc, RAC and Anne-Virginie Eggimann, MSc
6. Working as a Self-employed Independent Consultant 45
   By Robert Myers, PhD
7. Is a Career in a Large, Global Pharmaceutical Company Right for You? ... 53
   By Bonnie J. Goldmann, MD
8. Working in a Large Pharmaceutical Company 61
   By Paul Gil, PhD, RAC
9. Small Company Perspective 69
   By Meredith Brown-Tuttle, RAC
10. Working at a Small Pharmaceutical Company 79
    By Scott Oglesby, PhD
11. Working for a Generic Drug Company 87
    By Mary Lou Freathy, JD
12. Specializing in Regulatory Chemistry, Manufacturing and Controls 95
    By Joseph Greer, RAC
13. A Career in Promotional Regulatory 103
    By Kimberly Carneal
14. Alternative Career Pathways in Regulatory 113
    By Theresa M. Straut, CIP, RAC
15. Regulatory Operations 119
    By Katie Ditton, RAC
16. Regulatory Intelligence 127
    By Linda Bowen, MS, RAC
17. Your Career as a Biopharmaceutical Regulatory Writer 133
    By Nancy R. Katz, PhD
18. How I Got Into Regulatory 145
    By Christine Conroy

Table of Contents

19. How I Got Started in Regulatory 149
    By Evangeline D. Loh, PhD, RAC
20. How I Got Started in Regulatory 153
    By Meredith Brown-Tuttle, RAC
21. Paving the Way to a Regulatory Career—How I Got Started 155
    By Stephanie Anderson
22. How I Got Started in Regulatory 159
    By Nancy Pire Smerkanich
23. How I Got Started in Regulatory 163
    By Linda Bowen, MS, RAC
24. How I Got Started in Regulatory 167
    By Amy Grant

Index 171
Acronyms 175

CHOOSING THE RIGHT REGULATORY CAREER

CHAPTER 1
Introduction

By Peggy Berry, MBA, RAC

The regulatory profession is not, in my opinion, one of those careers that kids dream about. In fact, most adults do not even know it exists or what regulatory professionals actually do. So, how do so many people end up in the regulatory profession? From my 20 years of experience in regulatory, I can report that the typical story about entering the profession begins: "It happened by accident…" or words to that effect. In this book, you will find similar stories from a variety of professionals.

Furthermore, regulatory can be entered from many different directions. Like spokes on a bicycle wheel that converge on a central point, many paths lead to the profession. Most professionals have a scientific background, but they may have worked in a research laboratory or a quality department, or as a university professor or a practicing physician before arriving in the regulatory arena. Educational credentials range from a bachelor's degree to a doctorate. There are no hard and fast rules about requirements for a career in regulatory, resulting in maximum flexibility for applicants and hiring organizations. This book is structured to provide insights, considerations, tips and ideas for both new and seasoned regulatory professionals. You will find information about some of the more typical requirements for various levels and types of regulatory positions.

There are a number of different aspects of regulatory work that attract an individual to this profession. One is the variety of activities and areas available. At the macro level, one may work with branded or generic pharmaceuticals sold by prescription or over the counter, with biologics or with medical devices that are new or substantially equivalent devices. One may perform regulatory duties at global or regional companies of any size. In addition, the company or the professional may focus on a specific therapeutic area. In this book, you will read about the experiences of regulatory professionals working in various types of organizations and different product areas. The authors also compare and contrast these work areas and organizational types with their own experiences, and share guidance and tips.

Another consideration for regulatory professionals is whether to specialize in areas such as chemistry, manufacturing and controls, advertising or labeling, or to remain a generalist. Several of the authors describe requirements for specialization and the benefits of doing so, as well as their own career choices. Each specialty area, type of company and product development sector has characteristics that are more or less appealing to each individual.

Personally, I have worked for the government, contract research organizations, biotechnology companies and small and large pharmaceutical firms. I have specialized in one area and otherwise been a generalist. In gaining all of these experiences, I learned that that I prefer working at small to medium-sized companies because I like performing a large variety of tasks and having a clear, visible impact on a given project or organization. I also am inclined toward change and continuous improvement and find fulfillment in changing jobs every four years or so. New roles allow me to learn from other professionals—within regulatory and other areas of the company—and gain new and diverse experiences that expand my overall regulatory knowledge.

There are three lessons that I have found most valuable throughout my career.

Listen and Learn

No matter what you are doing or how long you have been doing it, you will always get further ahead if you listen to those around you and adjust your response or reaction accordingly. I find that listening is one of the most effective tools that a regulatory professional can master. It helps in dealing with project teams, senior management, direct reports, contractors, consultants and FDA or other regulatory authorities. Every person comes into a situation with a certain set of biases and assumptions. It is important to intentionally minimize your own biases and challenge your own assumptions to be open to and fully aware of other people's perspective—whether you ultimately agree with it or not. Learning this skill will be helpful early in your career to fully understand what is expected of you, and it will be helpful later for many reasons, including fully understanding the regulatory agency's viewpoint and priorities.

Introduction

There is a certain amount of passive learning that accompanies listening in the situations described above. But there is much more learning that can be done actively by the regulatory professional, including researching those you are doing business with, your direct competitors and so on. In addition, I would emphasize that to be the most successful regulatory professional possible, you should become a sponge for any and all information. Do not filter your learning because you think information is not relevant to your current job or company. Learn from every interaction and every situation. Over the years, I have found that I can learn something from every person whom I encounter. In some cases, it may be a technical skill such as creating an animation in PowerPoint or an xml file for a Common Technical Document (CTD), or a less-tangible skill such as how adults learn best. Everything you learn can eventually be used to help you advance your career, be a better person or build a better relationship in the future.

Ask Anyone Anything

My next piece of advice is to seize every opportunity to learn more. Just as children always ask "Why?", so should you. Ask finance: "Why do you need this report? What do you do with it? Why does the SEC require it and does it apply to all companies or just ours?" Ask your boss: "What is the best way to present the accomplishments of the organization? Is there a specific way the CEO or the board wants to see the information? What is most important to the CEO or the board? How can I help you do your job better? Why did the company decide not to pursue that partnership or that deal?" I have found that virtually everyone wants to teach you about what they do and why they do it—you just have to be willing to ask, listen and learn. I have also found there is very little that is off limits. I would say that in 20 years of asking about 500 people more than a million questions, I can count on two hands the number of times that someone said, "I can't tell you that information."

Asking questions also builds relationships. When you ask people about their work and they share with you and teach you, you are adding people with a variety of skills and a vast amount of knowledge to your own personal network. Having a large group of "go-to" people can help you later when you need resources they possess.

Never Say No

Not only do I suggest you never say no, in fact, I think you should seek out opportunities to volunteer or take on additional responsibilities. This does not mean that you should work 20 hours a day and have no life outside work in order to advance. However, it does mean you should volunteer to help anyone who needs assistance with his or her job, even if it means staying late or coming in early. For example, if you notice that regulatory operations is preparing a big submission, ask whether there is anything you can do to help, even if operations is not your job or you have never done it before. Often, you can check links and bookmarks or perform a quality check on documents and, in the process, learn about putting together a submission and how FDA might navigate that submission. You might also volunteer for special projects you have the skills or ability to complete so you can gain additional experience or build better relationships.

For example, about 15 years ago, I volunteered to build a major database that would be used by the entire company to track a certain type of document, actions required, responsibilities, responses and other key items. It took about three weeks to build the comprehensive database and teach several users how to input information into the system. The database was in use for about 10 years and the heads of the impacted units never forgot I had stepped in and volunteered to give them a tool to make their jobs easier and made them more efficient. To this day, I can call those individuals for information or advice and they occasionally still refer to how that database helped them.

Another aspect of this advice is to always try to do the work of the next position you want. When an opportunity arises that will allow you to take on more responsibility within your own department, even if it is only temporary, take it—every small step will lead you closer to the position you want. During my own career, I often boldly requested more responsibility and opportunity and was frequently rewarded for taking the chance, including getting more responsibility, gaining additional learning and experience outside my specific job function and, ultimately, receiving promotions or being sought after for highly visible projects. The worst that could happen is for someone to say you are not quite ready or they have chosen someone else this time.

For example, I worked for a company whose projects were led by PhD professionals. When there were too many projects for the available PhD project leaders, the company had to decide whether to postpone a project, give too many projects to a single leader or hire another project leader who would then have too few projects. Recognizing this dilemma, I went to the president of the company and said that I wanted the opportunity to lead the project. I told him why this would be a good choice; what experience, skills and abilities I brought to the table; what I was willing to do to get the job done; and what I would do to get mentoring in the areas where I did not have enough information or needed some guidance. In view of my self-confidence and the plan I presented, I became the first non-PhD project leader for the company. I still had to fulfill all my

Introduction

regulatory functions and did not receive a promotion or more money. However, it was one of the best choices I ever made because I learned a lot about leadership, management, overall drug development, providing relevant information to senior management, and guiding a project team to get a job done.

So, seek out opportunities, ask for what you want or what you think would be beneficial, show how you can contribute and never say no in the face of an opportunity—and you will expand your possibilities and find new choices.

There are at least 100 other pieces of advice or wisdom or learning I could share, but most of them would all circle back to the three I have mentioned. I strongly believe you are in control of your own career; you can shape it and, with some creative thought and consideration, you can shape your world to achieve what you want.

This book can be a step in your journey. Read what others have been through, learn from their experiences, consider their advice and ponder their thoughts. Discuss these things with your colleagues or your supervisor to gain additional insights. If you have more questions, take my advice and ask anyone anything—reach out to the authors, ask them for more information about what they do, extend your network to include them, meet up with them at a RAPS conference or connect through LinkedIn. Do not manufacture constraints for yourself—others will do that. Instead, remember that you can talk to anyone, learn anything, and break any boundaries. This confidence will open a new world of ideas and opportunities you could never have planned.

Good luck in your career!

CHAPTER 2

Support Groups and Organizations for Regulatory Professionals

By Amy Grant

Support groups and organizations offer many benefits to regulatory professionals. People find great value in networking and sharing nonproprietary information and experience. There are many opportunities to specialize and deepen one's knowledge of regulatory and to learn and improve in general. Collaborations in groups and organizations have produced benefits such as standards for technology, revisions and clarification of regulations and guidelines and critical path initiatives ultimately resulting in innovative medicines for patients. Support groups and organizations offer opportunities for leadership, development and mentoring; all of which enhance a regulatory professional's skills and practices.

Support groups are informal networks of people that may or may not be part of a formal professional organization. Support groups may be formed within or outside the workplace and may involve people with common interests who meet informally on a regular basis to discuss their challenges and experiences.

Professional organizations are formalized bodies with a common interest or purpose. Some professional organizations may also have support groups and activities such as special interest groups, workshops and local chapters, and activities that offer benefits to smaller subgroups of the membership.

Working in regulatory requires innovative thinking; interpretation of laws, regulations and guidelines; and experience-based decision making. Support groups and organizations provide educational forums for discussion and consideration of basic regulations and guidelines from local, regional and international perspectives. For example, support groups and organizations provide neutral ground for government, academia, industry, healthcare providers, patients and others to share ideas to enhance understanding of new pediatric/ pediatric regulations and guidances, orphan product designation and new legislation. Regulatory professionals take what they learn at these educational forums and apply it confidentially to specific situations.

It is important for members of support groups and organizations to follow codes of conduct and ethics and to have a clear understanding of proprietary versus nonproprietary information, i.e., what is in the private versus the public domain.

Regulatory is a multidisciplinary field with close ties to other disciplines including clinical; legal; chemistry, manufacturing and controls (CMC); project management; medical affairs; promotional regulatory affairs; marketing; and Quality Assurance. Through support groups and organizations, participants have opportunities for discussion across cultures, geographic locations, disciplines and various sectors in the biopharmaceutical community such as academia, government, healthcare, legal, payers, patients and others with a vested interest in developing medicines. Multiple perspectives and lessons learned help regulatory professionals apply regulations and guidelines in context, while being both focused on the future and historically savvy.

Examples of Support Groups and Organizations

Examples of regulatory professional organizations include:
- The Regulatory Affairs Professional Society (RAPS) RAPS.org
- The Drug Information Association (DIA) www.diahome.org
- The Organisation for Professionals in Regulatory Affairs (TOPRA) www.topra.org/.

All three organizations are educational, nonprofit and nongovernmental and offer membership worldwide with various benefits including publications, education and training, conferences, career development and other products and benefits.

RAPS is the largest international membership organization for all regulatory professionals in the healthcare product sector, including those involved in medical devices, pharmaceuticals, biotechnology and other healthcare products. RAPS supports Regulatory Affairs Certification (RAC), the only professional credential specifically for the healthcare regulatory profession, sets ethical standards, and conducts research on the profession, including its biannual *Regulatory Scope of Practice and Compensation Report*. RAPS has 12,000 members in more than 50 countries. It is headquartered near Washington, DC, with offices in Brussels and Tokyo.

In DIA, regulatory is one section of the larger organization. Per its website, DIA has 18,000 members involved in the discovery, development, regulation, surveillance or marketing of pharmaceuticals or related products. TOPRA is based in the UK and has members drawn from more than 40 countries.

There are also regional groups and organizations focused on specialties in regulatory. The North Carolina Regulatory Affairs Forum (NCRAF www.ncraf.org/) is an example of a regional group. The Parenteral Drug Association (PDA www.pda.org/) has more than 10,000 members worldwide and has a specialty group focusing on regulatory science and technology. The International Society for Pharmaceutical Engineering (ISPE www.ispe.org) has 25,000 pharmaceutical science and manufacturing members from more than 90 countries and features Product Quality Lifecycle Implementation (PQLI) that helps industry find practical, global approaches to implementing ICH guidances. The Special Libraries Association (SLA www.sla.org/) has an active pharmaceutical and health technology division focused on information science (http://units.sla.org/division/dpht/). These organizations and groups within organizations also enhance the regulatory profession through education and communication and provide opportunities for personal and professional growth.

Industry trade organizations also provide formal and informal opportunities for regulatory professionals. Examples include: the Biotechnology Industry Organization (BIO www.bio.org/) the European Federation of Pharmaceutical Industries and Associations (EFPIA www.efpia.org/Content/Default.asp) the International Federation of Pharmaceutical Manufacturers and Associations (IFPMA www.ifpma.org/) and the Pharmaceutical Research and Manufacturers of America (PhRMA www.phrma.org/) Company representatives participate in formal committee and informal working groups including regulatory sections. Participation offers opportunities to hear multiple points of view and to contribute comments on emerging policies, regulations and guidance documents. Involvement also enhances personal and professional communication skills.

It is important to discover which group and/or organization has the most value for you and your company given your current job, location and interests. With the help of your manager, find the mutual benefit and balance between your personal development needs and what is most important to the company. Decide what is needed, e.g., practical information, networking and/or personal development. Considerations include membership fees, volunteer opportunities, strengths and weaknesses of the external organization and potential career development opportunities. By attending programs and talking with members, you can quickly learn if there is a fit with the support group or organization.

Most organizations offer discounted memberships for students plus introductory programs. Organizations also provide advanced training for seasoned regulatory professionals.

Groups and organizations offer many diverse volunteer opportunities. For example, if networking in person is important, you could become active in a local chapter of an organization. You could plan in advance to attend an annual meeting and make arrangements for informal and formal face-to-face meetings. If leadership development is important, you could become involved in committees, boards and election of officers. In addition, support groups and organizations offer many opportunities to develop skills such as public speaking, training and presentation development.

Volunteer activities can require a significant time commitment. Serving on a board, chairing programs at annual meetings and writing and publishing require careful planning and discussions with your manager and others, e.g., corporate communications lead. It is important to find a balance between the time you spend at work, at home and performing volunteer activities for support groups and organizations. For example, would you be able to apply what you learn from your volunteer activity if you spend one hour a month on a teleconference as part of a working group on a topic of importance to your company? Would the benefits of a face-to-face working group that requires additional time and travel outweigh the downside of time spent volunteering? Is there a fit between your goals at work and your volunteer work in the support group and/or organization?

Conclusion

Nonprofit educational organizations can offer significant opportunities for learning and involvement as well as networking. They are also dedicated to the professionals that they serve and are independent of commercial influence. For example, RAPS, DIA, TOPRA, PDA, NCRAF and SLA strive to be nonpolitical, so, interaction among academia, industry, government, healthcare and other groups takes place in a neutral forum. Trade organizations, ICH and WHO are focused on policies and advocacy and have different legal frameworks, requirements and cultures. Take time to determine what you and your company need. Explore and consider the weaknesses and strengths of each organization and plan accordingly.

References

Biotechnology Industry Organization. BIO website. www.bio.org. Accessed 17 August 2010.
DeVinne P, ed. *The American Heritage Dictionary*. 2nd college ed. Boston, MA: Houghton Mifflin Company; 1985.
European Federation of Pharmaceutical Industries and Associations. EFPIA website. www.efpia.org/Content/Default.asp. Accessed 17 August 2010.
International Federation of Pharmaceutical Manufacturers & Associations. IFPMA website. www.ifpma.org/. Accessed 17 August 2010.
International Society for Pharmaceutical Engineering. ISPE website. www.ispe.org. Accessed 17 August 2010.
The North Carolina Regulatory Affairs Forum. NCRAF website. www.ncraf.org/. Accessed 17 August 2010.
Parenteral Drug Association. PDA website. www.pda.org/. Accessed 17 August 2010.
Pharmaceutical Research and Manufacturers of America. PhRMA website. www.phrma.org/. Accessed 17 August 2010.
Regulatory Affairs Professionals Society. RAPS website. www.RAPS.org. Accessed 17 August 2010.
Regulatory Affairs Professionals Society, 2010 Scope of Practice & Compensation Report for the Regulatory Profession
The Special Libraries Association. Pharmaceutical and Health Technology Division website. www.sla.org/ and http://units.sla.org/division/dpht/. Accessed 17 August 2010.
The Organisation for Professionals in Regulatory Affairs. TOPRA website. www.topra.org/. Accessed 17 August 2010.

Chapter 3
Education

By Kathryn Davidson, RAC

Two major aspects of regulatory are comprised of two separate functions: regulatory affairs and regulatory operations. They involve different responsibilities and, subsequently, have different educational requirements and opportunities.

Regulatory Affairs (RA)

Regulatory professionals under the RA function are responsible for setting submission strategy and determining what must be submitted to meet reporting requirements and demonstrate that the product is safe and effective.

Historically, new RA personnel learned by reading applicable legislative and guidance documents, receiving on-the-job training from someone with more experience, and attending conferences. However, as scientific knowledge has increased, so has the amount of information that must be submitted to regulatory authorities and, subsequently, the number of legislative and guidance documents. RA personnel must now be involved in all aspects of product development to ensure that regulatory reporting requirements are met.

Educational offerings for RA include certification, certificate and degree programs, conferences, webinars and professional organizations. More details on opportunities in each educational area are provided below.

Certification

In 1990, the Regulatory Affairs Professionals Society (RAPS) introduced

Regulatory Affairs Certification (RAC) to recognize the level of knowledge attained by regulatory professionals. The first RAC certification addressed laws, regulations, policies and guidelines for healthcare products marketed in the US. An RAC focusing on regulatory requirements for the EU market was introduced in 2001 and an RAC for Canada followed in 2004. The newest addition, the RAC (General Scope), covers regulatory functions throughout the healthcare product lifecycle as well as international standards and guidelines, and was introduced in 2009. To qualify to take any of the certification examinations, the candidate must have either a bachelor's degree (or equivalent) or three to five years of regulatory experience. Each exam consists of 100 multiple-choice questions that must be completed in two hours. The examinations may be taken during a two-month window offered in the spring and autumn. Examination results are made available to candidates within four weeks after the close of the exam window. Books, courses and other aids are offered for exam preparation. Practice examinations are particularly helpful as they identify areas of focus and familiarize the candidate with the format of questions (double negatives are not uncommon). Once a credential is achieved, recertification every three years is required by earning "points" through such activities as attending or speaking at conferences or classes, participating in professional organizations, writing articles or engaging in activities that "further the profession."

Certificate Programs

To fill the increasing need for RA training, certificate programs were introduced by professional organizations and universities/colleges. Certificates are offered at various levels, with corresponding educational background requirements ranging from no degree to a master's degree. Certificate programs may be independent offerings or available in conjunction with a master's degree program.

Independent Certificate Programs

The following independent certificate programs do not offer a path toward a degree program.
- RAPS offers three regulatory affairs certificates through its Online University with concentrations in medical devices and pharmaceuticals, as well as a dual program that combines key elements of both. All courses required to earn the certificate are self-paced and can be accessed online at any time; there are no required prerequisites. The medical devices and pharmaceuticals programs consist of four core courses and five electives that students must complete in six months. The dual program consists of six core courses and eight

EDUCATION

electives that students must complete is one year. RAPS.org/onlineu.

- The Center for Professional Innovation & Education (CfPIE) offers a Global Regulatory Affairs Compliance Professional (GRACP) certificate. Candidates should have an undergraduate degree. Participants select three core courses and one elective. Each course is one to two days in length. Classes are situated near major airports to accommodate working professionals. (www.cfpie.com/showitem.aspx?productid=GRACP)
- The University of Washington Extension (Bellevue, WA) offers a certificate in biomedical regulatory affairs. Candidates must have a bachelor's degree or relevant work experience in the biomedical field. Students take three classes (Introduction to Biomedical Regulatory Affairs; Product Development and Manufacturing Systems; and Product Testing, Evaluation and Postmarket Issues). One class is offered per quarter on Tuesday nights starting each autumn. (www.extension.washington.edu/ext/certificates/bio/bio_gen.asp)
- San Diego State University offers a certificate in regulatory affairs that is available completely online. Candidates must have an undergraduate degree. The program is comprised of four courses: The Pharmaceutical, Biotechnology and Device Industries; Introduction to Food and Drug Law; Current Good Manufacturing Practice—General Concepts; and Practical Ethics for Healthcare Professionals. (http://interwork.sdsu.edu/cbbd/regaffairs/adv_cert.htm)
- Seneca College of Applied Arts and Technology in Toronto, Canada, offers the Pharmaceutical Regulatory Affairs & Quality Operations Graduate Certificate. Candidates must have completed an undergraduate science degree. The certificate requires completion of 10 classes that are offered on a semester basis in the evening for 14 weeks or weekends (Saturdays from 9:00 am–4:00 pm) for seven weeks. (www.senecac.on.ca/ce/programs/pharma_regulatory.html)
- Hood College (Frederick, MD) offers a 15-credit, graduate-level certificate program in regulatory compliance consisting of five courses (Good Laboratory Practice; Product Development; Good Manufacturing Practice; Development of Pharmaceuticals and Regulatory Environment; and Good Clinical Practice). Worth three credits each, the classes are offered on a semester basis. (www.hood.edu/academics/certificate.cfm?pid=certificate_regulatory.html)
- Lehigh University offers a 12-credit, graduate-level certificate program entitled Regulatory Affairs in a Technical Environment. To be eligible,

candidates must have a background in analytical chemistry and have completed two semesters of organic chemistry and one semester of biochemistry. All classes are offered online on a semester basis. Students must arrange for an independent proctor for examinations. The classes, which have a heavy chemistry emphasis, are: Regulatory I Discovery to Approval; Regulatory II Biomarkers; Regulatory III Validation of Analytical Assays; Regulatory IV Commercial Production; Validation and Process Qualification; and Regulatory V Pharmaceutics. Students must complete four of five courses to earn the certificate. (www.distance.lehigh.edu/credit/cert_regulatory_affairs.htm)

- Northeastern University College of Professional Studies, with campuses in the Boston area, offers two, 16-quarter-hour, graduate-level certificate programs in biopharmaceutical regulatory affairs (domestic (US) and international). Classes are offered online. The Domestic Certificate requires three core courses (Biologics Development, New Drug Development and Medical Device Development) and one elective. (www.cps.neu.edu/gradcert_domestic/)

    The International Certificate requires two core courses (Global Biotechnology Product Registration and European Union Compliance Process and Regulatory Affairs) and two electives. (www.cps.neu.edu/gradcert_internat/)

- Temple University offers a post-master's certificate in advanced regulatory affairs. Temple University alumni graduating with a masters' degree in Quality Assurance (QA)/RA must complete four courses. Candidates who completed their master of science degree elsewhere must also have worked in the pharmaceutical industry in a specific specialty for at least 10 years and are required to complete five courses to earn the certificate. There are 51 courses in advanced regulatory affairs from which to choose. Classes are offered on evenings and weekends on a semester basis at one of Temple's three campuses (Fort Washington, PA, Frazer, PA and Tarrytown, NY). In some cases, arrangements can be made for corporate sites to host or videoconference the classes. (www.temple.edu/pharmacy_qara/pdf/brochure_Post-MastersCertificates.pdf)

    Graduates of Temple University's master's program in QA/RA are also eligible to participate in three other post-master's certificate programs. The Post-Master's Certificate in Medical Devices requires completion of four of six possible courses. The Post-Master's Certificate in GMPs for the 21st Century requires completion of five courses of six offered. The Post-Master's Certificate in Biopharmaceuticals and Generic Drugs requires completing four of five courses offered (www.temple.edu/pharmacy_qara/certificates.htm#advdevices).

Certificates Offered in Conjunction With a Master's Degree Program

Many of the universities that offer master's degrees also offer certificate programs. The classes are the same for both the certificate and the master's programs; however, the admissions and coursework completion criteria are different. The following certificate programs are offered by educational institutions that also offer graduate degree programs in RA.

- The Organisation for Professionals in Regulatory Affairs (TOPRA) offers a postgraduate certificate (PgCert) through the Cranfield University. Students complete five of eight of the courses required for the master of science degree in medical technology regulatory affairs. (www.topra.org/postgraduate-qualifications/msc-medical-technology-regulatory-affairs/course-structure)
- Purdue University offers a graduate certificate program in regulatory and quality compliance consisting of three courses, each worth three credit hours. The classes (US Food and Drug Law, Drug Discovery and Development, and Good Regulatory (GXP) Practices) are offered on a semester basis. Classes are conducted on one weekend per month (from Friday afternoon through midday on Sunday at the West Lafayette, IN campus. (www.ipph.purdue.edu/graduateprogram/cert-rqc/)
- Temple University offers seven certificates—Drug Development, Clinical Trial Management, Medical Devices, Basic Pharmaceutical Development, Good Manufacturing Practices (GMPs) for the 21st Century, and Biopharmaceuticals and Generic Drugs—that may be earned independently or as an intermediate step to achieving the master's degree in regulatory affairs. If students are working toward the master's degree, they may only earn one certificate. The Drug Development certificate requires completion of two core classes, a GXP course and a QA/RA elective. The Clinical Trial Management certificate requires completion of five core courses. The Medical Devices certificate requires completion of four core courses and one QA/RA elective. The Basic Pharmaceutical Development certificate, for students with a nonscientific background, requires completion of two core courses and two QA/RA electives. The GMPs for the 21st Century certificate requires completion of five core courses. The Biopharmaceuticals and Generic Drugs certificate requires completion

of four core courses. More information on the certificate programs is available at www.temple.edu/pharmacy_qara/certificates.htm.
- The University of Georgia College of Pharmacy offers a certificate that is a subset of classes from its master of science in pharmacy program with an emphasis on regulatory affairs. The application process and admission criteria are separate for the certificate and master's; however, courses used to complete the certificate will count toward the master's should a student decide to pursue the degree. Classes are offered at the Gwinnett, GA, campus on a part-time basis for working professionals. At this writing, the master of science program was being revised and consequently, requirements for neither the certificate nor the degree were clearly defined (www.rx.uga.edu/main/home/reg_affairs/program_description.htm).

Master's Degrees

There are a number of options available for those interested in pursuing a master's in regulatory affairs or in another discipline with an emphasis on RA. The offerings have been grouped based upon geographic restrictions.

On Campus Only
- John Hopkins University offers two master's degrees in regulatory affairs. Courses are primarily offered in the evening (some are available on weekends or online) at the Homewood Campus in Baltimore, MD, the Montgomery County Campus in Rockville, MD, or the HEAT Center in Aberdeen, MD. Students can choose courses offered in an online "wet" lab, which is equipped with spectrophotometric devices, capillary electrophoresis for DNA and protein analysis, computerized gel image analyzer and cell culture fermentation units. (www.advanced.jhu.edu/contact/campuses/montgomery/vtour-mcc/wetlab/vtour-MCC-wetlab.html)

    The master of science in bioscience regulatory affairs encompasses six core courses, three electives and a practicum hands-on course. (http://advanced.jhu.edu/academic/biotechnology/bioscience/requirements/)

    The master of science in biotechnology with an emphasis on regulatory affairs requires completion of 10 courses, six of which must be in science. (http://advanced.jhu.edu/academic/biotechnology/biotech/requirements/#regulatoryaffairs)
- The Keck Graduate Institute of Applied Life Sciences in Claremont,

EDUCATION

CA offers a masters of bioscience with a concentration in clinical and regulatory affairs. The program is full time for two years with a mandatory summer internship. (http://aboldnewhybrid.kgi.edu/master_of_bioscience.php)

- Long Island University's Arnold and Marie Schwartz College of Pharmacy offers a master of science in drug regulatory affairs. Students may select either a thesis option (30 credits of coursework with six credits for research and thesis) or a non-thesis option (33 credits and a passing mark on a comprehensive written examination). www.liu.edu/cwis/pharmacy/phbut07/grad03.html#4)
- The Massachusetts College of Pharmacy offers a master of science in regulatory affairs and health policy (RAHP). Candidates must provide GRE scores if they graduated in the previous five years. All classes are offered on the Boston campus. Students must complete nine courses and a written graduate case study thesis (graded pass/fail) for a total of 30 semester hours. (www.mcphs.edu/academics/programs/pharmaceutical%5Fsciences/regulatory%5Faffairs/)
- The Northeastern University College of Professional Studies offers a master of science in regulatory affairs for drugs, biologics and medical devices. Courses are offered at night at the Boston campus and online. Six core courses, one elective course, and one course each in business, safety and marketing are required to complete the program. www.cps.neu.edu/ms_reg/)
- Purdue University in West Lafayette, IN, offers master of science degrees in regulatory and quality compliance. A minimum of 67 units must be completed, with the largest concentration of classes in nuclear medicine (including two clerkships). (www.ipph.purdue.edu/graduateprogram/ms-rqc/)
- St. Cloud State University's master of science in regulatory affairs and services (RAS) program focuses solely on medical devices. The program consists of 11 courses for a total of 33 units that include a culminating project. All classes are held at the College of Science and Engineering campus in Brooklyn Park, MN. (www.stcloudstate.edu/ras/home.asp)
- Temple University School of Pharmacy offers master's degrees in QA and RA. The program has four core courses totaling 12 credits (Drug Development, Food and Drug Law, a Good Practices course (Good Manufacturing Practice (GMP), Good Clinical Practice (GCP), Good Laboratory Practice (GLP) or Advanced GMP), and Quality

Audit or Investigational New Drug (IND)/ New Drug Application (NDA) Submissions), and students must complete an additional eight electives (24 credits) for a total of 36 credits. All courses are available at both the Fort Washington, PA, and Tarrytown, NY, campuses. Classes are offered in two formats: one-night per week for 10–12 weeks or five to six all-day classes on either Saturday or Sunday. The entire program can be completed by taking just the weekend classes. (www.temple.edu/pharmacy_qara/)

- The University of Georgia College of Pharmacy offers a master of science in pharmacy with an emphasis in regulatory affairs. Classes are offered at the Gwinnett, GA, campus on a part-time basis because the program is oriented toward working professionals. At this writing, the program was being revised and consequently, requirements were not clearly defined. (www.rx.uga.edu/main/home/reg_affairs/program_description.htm)
- The Organisation for Professionals in Regulatory Affairs (TOPRA) offers two master of science degree programs designed for working professionals with participation on a part-time basis only. Candidates for either program should have an undergraduate degree and at least two years of experience in RA. In special circumstances, substantial experience might substitute for a degree. The master of science in regulatory affairs is offered by TOPRA in London, and then validated and awarded by the University of Wales. Students must complete eight of 12 modules offered. The modules start with two and a half days of lectures, case studies and discussion groups, and require at least 80 hours of independent study to complete a course journal (collection and analysis of relevant reference materials) and two written assignments (one from a choice of three questions and the other a compulsory problem-based analysis) within four months. Students are also required to submit a research-based dissertation of 18,000–20,000 words and give a short, oral presentation on the dissertation to an audience of RA professionals. (www.topra.org/files/assets/pdf/MScProspectus07-08.pdf)
- TOPRA's master of science in medical technology regulatory affairs program is in collaboration with Cranfield Health Partnership at the Cranfield University campus in Bedfordshire, England. Students must complete eight modules (weighted as 50% of the program). The modules include three days of lectures, case studies and discussion groups and require additional, independent study to complete a course journal, case study and written assignments. Students must also complete a research

project culminating in a thesis (weighted as the other 50% of the program). Students may submit a dissertation instead of a thesis, but will receive a postgraduate diploma (PgDip) rather than a master's designation. (www.topra.org/files/assets/pdf/mtra.pdf)

Choice of On Campus or Online
- The Northeastern University College of Professional Studies offers two master of science programs relevant to regulatory. The master of science in regulatory affairs is offered online with some classes also offered at the Boston campus at night. The program requires 40 quarter hours with completion in two years expected, based upon taking two classes at a time. (www.cps.neu.edu/ms_reg/)

  The master of science in quality assurance and regulatory science is only offered at the Boston campus. More information is provided on this program in the section covering courses offered only on campus.

Online Only
- San Diego State University offers a master of science in regulatory affairs. The program requires completion of 39 units, 27 of which are required courses. Twelve units of electives must also be taken, with at least nine specific to regulatory and quality. (http://interwork.sdsu.edu/cbbd/regaffairs/ms_regaffairs.htm)
- The University of Southern California offers a master of science in regulatory science. Students must complete 36 units to graduate. Typically, students take 30 units of coursework (usually eight courses from seven focus areas plus two electives) and complete a six-unit internship/research project. Students with industry experience may be allowed to substitute six units of coursework for the internship or complete the research project in their workplace (the university cannot give credit for previous work experience). (http://regulatory.usc.edu/program_ms.aspx#)

Doctorates

The latest development in educational offerings is the availability of a doctorate in regulatory science, which is offered by the University of Southern California and is available entirely online. Students must complete 64 units with at least 15 units in foundational courses, eight units each in Product Lifecycle Strategy, Project and Personnel Management and Global Regulatory

Strategy and Policy, and 10 units in Research and Dissertation Preparation and Completion. Students must take a written examination after completing the foundational courses and prepare and defend an independent dissertation in order to graduate. (http://regulatory.usc.edu/program_drs.aspx).

Conferences and Webinars

Regulations and requirements are continuously being updated as new discoveries improve the ability to scientifically determine whether a product is safe and/or effective. Regulatory professionals must proactively follow these changes to make their companies aware of the new standards and ensure compliance. Conferences, webinars and professional organizations are all important tools in staying current.

Conferences and webinars are organized by many different organizations, some of which focus solely on providing educational services while others also provide professional membership services. Both types of organizations can provide valuable training. There are too many conferences and webinars to list here. An Internet search on your topic of choice will yield a number of results.

Professional Organizations

There are a variety of professional membership organizations, some highly specialized and others more general in focus. Some of the latter are RAPS, the Drug Information Association (DIA) and TOPRA.

Geographically focused organizations include the Canadian Association of Professional Regulatory Affairs (CAPRA) and the Pharmaceutical Sciences Group (also Canadian). Subject focused organizations include CASSS (formerly the California Separation Science Society) and the Parenteral Drug Association (PDA).

Regulatory Operations (RO)

Regulatory Operations (RO) has three discrete functions. These may either be performed by the same person (common in small companies) or further delineated into separate functional roles (more frequently seen in larger organizations). They are:
- Systems support—responsible for computer systems and technical support
- Publishing—responsible for formatting, publishing and sending submissions
- Document control—responsible for archiving submissions

For more information on these three areas, refer Chapter 15, "Regulatory Operations."

RO is still typically learned through on-the-job training. There are no formal certification, certificate or degree programs in the general knowledge area of RO. Highly specialized sub-area programs are available.

Certification

There are some highly specialized certification programs related to specific computer systems utilized in the submission process. For example, Thomson Reuters (formerly Liquent) offers separate certifications for users and administrators of its publishing systems. Image Solutions Inc. offers specialist and master's levels of certification for its ISIToolbox. Even if the candidate regularly uses the program, taking training courses prior to taking the certification exam is recommended in order to become familiar with the nomenclature utilized by the software company as well as learn more about how the certification exam will be organized and structured.

Learning more about RA will also benefit the RO professional because the work of the two groups is so intertwined. The RAC designation is currently the only certification for RA.

Systems support personnel may benefit from pursuing IT certifications, depending upon their level of involvement and responsibility for administration of the infrastructure as well as specialized systems.

Certificate and Degree Programs

There are no certificate or degree programs available in RO at the time of this writing. Individuals interested in specializing in document control (archival) in a large company may find a graduate degree in library science helpful.

Conferences and Webinars

In Europe, the DIA Annual EuroMeeting provides helpful information on RO. In North America, the most focused conference for RO professionals is the DIA-sponsored electronic Common Technical Document (eCTD) conference offered on the West Coast in the fall. The DIA Electronic Document Management (EDM) conference in the spring on the East Coast and the DIA Annual Conference also have relevant information for the RO professional.

Training on the eCTD is helpful for RO professionals and there are courses offered by a number of organizations, including RAPS, DIA and PTi International (www.pti-international.com/).

Systems support personnel benefit from a thorough knowledge and understanding of validation principles and practices. Courses, journals and training products offered by organizations such as the Institute of Validation Technology (IVT) are helpful.

Professional Organizations

Professional membership organizations that provide information relevant to all areas of RO include RAPS and DIA. Both have special interest groups that focus on areas of importance to RO, for example, eCTD and regulated product submissions (RPS, the next generation of eCTD).

An organization of interest to some RO professionals, particularly those attracted to a career in RO management, is the Project Management Institute. This group focuses on creating and managing project timelines, a skill essential to RO because timelines are frequently not allowed to slip even when critical information is delayed.

RO personnel involved in document control would be well served by joining the Association of Records Managers and Administrators (ARMA), an organization devoted to appropriate storage, retrieval and retention of information.

Conclusion

Educational opportunities in RA and RO are different. RA has formal educational opportunities including certifications and certificate and degree programs. RO remains largely dependent upon on-the-job training.

Chapter 4
Human Dynamics of Regulatory

By Amy Grant

The regulatory professional who is aware of human dynamics is in a position to make a positive impact, especially in coping with uncertainty and leading people through ambiguous situations and change. The social sciences provide insights into human dynamics. Drawing upon anthropology, economics, history, psychology, sociology and systems theory, I define "human dynamics" as a mixture of human attributes, actions and social networks interacting, interdependent and constantly moving in time. This mixture includes individuals and groups driven by various interests.

Definitions of and approaches to the study of human dynamics are diverse and subject to change. Others describe human dynamics as "fluid and reflective," "nonlinear and asynchronous" and "ripples in a pond."[1] In *The Sociological Imagination*, C.W. Mills relates human dynamics to variety, negotiation and multiple viewpoints. Amid this diversity of points of view, "A million little bargains are transacted every day, and everywhere there are more 'small groups' than anyone could ever count." Other lines of inquiry include learning in adulthood, gaming, choice, decision making, environmental factors, motivation, power, incentives and gender studies.[2] Some see humans as self determining while others focus on forces outside of human control.[3]

From a systems perspective, humans are dynamic rather than static and subject to forces contributing to both stability and change. Paradoxically, stability itself is dynamic despite the appearance of a steady state. As O'Connor and

McDermott write, "This is *dynamic equilibrium*. We cannot stand still even if we want to." Given this paradox, balance and an awareness of human dynamics are essential to the regulatory professional.

The human dynamics of regulatory are no different from those of other professions involving individuals and groups coping with information overload, change and stress. Workers have basic human needs such as described in Maslow's hierarchy: physiological; safety; love, affection, and belonging; esteem; and self-actualization.[4] For example, uncertainty about job status and pay has a direct impact on basic human physiological needs for food, clothing and shelter. Details such as the amount and type of light and temperature in work areas also have an impact on physiological needs.

Dynamic Equilibrium

In addition to basic human needs, other forces contribute to human dynamics. For example, the limitations of resources and time are constantly in play in the form of deadlines, and projects have interdependent moving parts with individuals and teams of people competing for resources. Human behaviors and attitudes are shaped by the push for increased speed, timing of events, and financial pressures. In general, humans are constantly in motion and seeking balance in the workplace and outside of work; known as dynamic equilibrium.

There are many examples of the principle of dynamic equilibrium in regulatory. A major challenge involves interpreting the "letter of the law" versus the "spirit of the law" in the context of various situations. In other words, what may appear to be absolute in the literal reading of the law (letter of the law) is not necessarily absolute in every situation and for every product (spirit of the law). And, one of the first things that regulatory professionals must understand is that laws and regulations are subject to interpretation—the extent of this understanding can separate good regulatory professionals from great regulatory professionals. Laws and regulations are not applied identically or interpreted in the same way by everyone, including companies and regulators, even though laws are intended to establish consistent rules. Laws tend to be written broadly and generally and are legally binding. Regulations are then written to provide additional information about interpretation and implementation standards and requirements under a specific law; they are also legally binding. Guidelines, including guides, US Food and Drug Administration (FDA) Manuals of Policies and Procedures (MaPPs), guidance documents, etc., are written to more precisely interpret the laws and regulations under specific circumstances or in certain situations. Guidelines are not legally binding but generally represent the current thinking of the agency and are expected to be followed in most circumstances.

It is important to be flexible and open to other perspectives when applying laws and rules to different situations. Remembering that people, and thereby, human dynamics, are involved in making an interpretation is critical. The interpretation of the subject at hand by each individual involved, which may disagree partially or completely with those of other individuals, is key to gaining an understanding of applicable requirements. Therefore, the importance of effectively communicating the reasoning and logic behind an interpretation of laws and rules cannot be overestimated. It is important to be aware of the specific audience and how to communicate effectively with them and across disciplines.

Effective communication can be challenging when team members do not have opportunities for face-to-face conversations or interactions. While email, teleconferences and video conferences provide alternative ways to communicate, they can decrease overall effectiveness and increase the need for repetition and follow-up. For example, intended meanings or emphasis and lack of comprehension that can be observed through body language in face-to-face interactions are lost in email and teleconferences. Additionally, there is an increased possibility for errors in translation or cultural uniqueness in communications to cause misunderstandings. For example, in using email, many individuals tend to be informal, direct and short, which may be interpreted by some as rudeness or lack of understanding, when in reality the individual is using a handheld device and trying to communicate with as few words as possible.

Successful regulatory professionals can recognize this and tactfully explore a problem without personalizing or polarizing the issue. For example, tensions can arise between US and EU teams trying to harmonize relatively well-defined data requirements. A good problem-solver will clarify the goal for the data, e.g., an approval submission in both the US and the EU, and then brainstorm with the team on how to meet the requirements of both regions.

When managed effectively, conflicting points of view can be highly positive: they can create healthy tension that prevents "group think" or domination of the discussion by one person. By exploring a variety of options, a well-considered decision can be made. However, when not managed effectively, disagreement and conflict can undermine a company with people pursuing their own personal wants and needs rather than implementing or supporting final decisions.

Changes, Choices and Cultural Influences

Other factors affect the human dynamics of regulatory. Shifts in disease areas, science, medicine, information technology and other areas have a major impact on the human dynamics of regulatory. Choices are made within a highly regulated, deadline-driven environment involving patient safety and serious and life-threatening diseases. Regulatory professionals come from diverse backgrounds and fields such as biology, chemistry, communications, computer science, nursing, law, literature, microbiology, pharmacy and physics. There are tensions and frictions when people with different perspectives and experiences interact under pressure. Each person brings a set of assumptions and experiences that color his perspective.

Cultural elements can also have a major impact on human interactions in regulatory. For example, one person's way of working may be different than another's. Language differences may necessitate a slower pace to ensure effective communication and comprehension. People who prefer a quicker pace may perceive the time needed by others as an obstacle and become frustrated, even though the time could provide the opportunity for better solutions and results. Some individuals prefer structured problem analysis and thoroughly considered resolution, which can take a bit of time, while others prefer to intuitively and rapidly implement a solution, which can be quite alarming for those regulatory professionals who prefer structure.

Regulatory professionals interact in complex situations and environments within and outside companies that often demand attention to both the details and the broader picture at the same time, e.g., local laws and the global guidelines.

Seasoned regulatory professionals are able to provide targeted and realistic analyses and interpretations of new and evolving legislation, regulations and guidance documents. The regulatory professional is in a unique position to have a positive impact on the company's decision making and bottom line by following these developments, assessing impact to the company's projects and advising about appropriate actions.

The pressures and stress often present in the regulatory workplace can bring out the best or the worst in people, depending upon personality and experience. For example, some people will seek solutions when others are paralyzed by the same situations. Some team members will listen to, challenge and ultimately accept regulatory strategies or advice and associated requirements that are provided by the regulatory professional, while others will go around the project leader or team to "opinion shop" through the chain of command or other individuals to seek the answer that they want to hear or gain agreement to proceed in a manner different from the advice of the regulatory professional. This opinion-shopping dynamic is often seen in workplaces where there is excessive competition among individuals or groups. In this type of setting, personal power is emphasized instead of the socialized power of teams and the company as a whole. Adding to the drive toward personal power is the genuine desire to bring forward products that will help people lead better lives. Regulatory professionals and others may have good intentions but may act without anticipating the consequences in organizations operating in the personal power dynamic.

In a workplace that emphasizes socialized power instead of personal power, the regulatory team leader does not need to constantly look good or receive credit in order to be accepted by peers or succeed professionally. In *The Fifth Discipline: The Art & Practice of the Learning Organization,* Peter Senge describes this dynamic of socialized power and how people decide to work together toward common goals. The leader is satisfied to contribute to the high-quality design of the project and does not need to take credit. The team has a sense of accomplishment, i.e., "We did this ourselves." In this type of workplace, people "do not behave as individual, isolated actors but as members of social networks."[5]

Because of the complexity of the regulatory profession, a workplace that emphasizes teamwork and capitalizes on the skills of its members will be the most effective. One person cannot know everything or work in isolation. Yet, one person can make a difference by bringing unique skills, experiences, insights and perspectives to the group. Acknowledgement that everyone matters may lead to greater personal security and confidence and empower the individual to feel his or her needs and goals are met when team and company needs and goals are met. Additionally, when people realize they can depend upon one another and themselves, they are less afraid to ask for help, take responsibility for errors and seek opportunities for innovation and improvement.

Regulatory departments tend to interact with all other departments, including all development departments, research, legal, corporate communications, investor relations, information technology and finance, as well as with executive management. Therefore, for effective communication, it is important for a regulatory professional to consider different points of view and understand the needs or contributions of each department. For example, in communicating regulatory risks, executive management may be most interested in the highest-probability risks that will delay approval; legal may be interested in the highest probability risks that will increase the company's liability, either to shareholders or to patients; finance may be interested in risks with the highest potential budget impact, etc. Knowing what is important to each department will enable better assessments of what risks to communicate.

Given the human dynamics outlined above, an effective regulatory professional needs the following skills:
- ability to identify, analyze, interpret and communicate regulatory risks

- ability to provide perspective to the team and consider other perspectives to achieve better solutions
- effective communication, including listening and other interpersonal skills, and an awareness of human dynamics

Future Focus

Regulatory work has both immediate and long-term impact on a submission's success, and the stakes are high for patients and families. Regulatory professionals are pressed to remain aware of the past, stay up to date on the latest developments and to anticipate the future. Per Peter Senge, "The systems perspective tells us that we must look beyond individual mistakes or bad luck to understand important problems. We must look beyond personalities and events. We must look into the underlying structures which shape individual actions and create the conditions where types of events become likely." In this ever-changing mix, essential skills for regulatory include setting realistic expectations, listening, maintaining balance and focus, negotiating with and influencing others and communicating. A "can do" attitude and flexibility to cope with ambiguity and the rapid pace of change globally and locally are also important.

The most valuable regulatory professionals are able to understand the goals of the company, including the commercial needs and value of the product, understand the requirements and needs of regulators globally and merge these viewpoints into valuable input into the development and commercial pathway for a product.

References
1. Merriam SB, Caffarella RS, Baumgartner LM. *Learning in Adulthood*. 3rd ed. San Francisco, CA: Jossey-Bass; 2007, p.11; Goldhaber DE. *Theories of Human Development: Integrative Perspectives*. London, England: Mayfield Publishing Co.; 2000, p.177; Morgan G. Images of Organization. London, England: Sage Publications; 2006, p. ix.
2. Levitt SD, Dubner SJ. *Freakonomics: A Rogue Economist Explores the Hidden Side of Everything*. Revised and Expanded Edition. New York, NY: HarperCollins; 2006, p. 11; Merriam SB, Caffarella RS, Baumgartner LM. *Learning in Adulthood*. 3rd ed. San Francisco, CA: Jossey-Bass; 2007, pp. 63-64, 339; Senge PM. *The Fifth Discipline: The Art & Practice of the Learning Organization*. New York, NY: DoubleDay; 2006, pp. 129 -130.
3. Frankl VE. *Man's Search for Meaning: An Introduction to Logotherapy*. 3rd ed. New York, NY: Simon and Schuster; 1984, p. 135-134.
4. Maslow AH. *Toward a Psychology of Being*. 3rd ed. New York, NY: John Wiley & Sons; 1999, pp. 65,168-70.
5. Senge PM. *The Fifth Discipline: The Art & Practice of the Learning Organization*. New York, NY: DoubleDay; 2006.

Chapter 5

Working as an Independent Regulatory Consultant

By Helene Sou, MSc, RAC and Anne-Virginie Eggimann, MSc

An "independent consultant" is broadly defined as a person who is self-employed and works for clients in a specific field on a per-project basis. In this introduction, we provide a description of the general roles of an independent regulatory consultant.

Independent consultants in regulatory work on a large variety of projects that can range in size, scope and duration depending upon the client's needs and the consultant's expertise and availability. In general, an independent consultant works on several clients' projects concurrently and must be able to handle projects with different requirements, budgets and timelines and different levels of commitment, from *ad hoc* questions to management to strategic oversight of large projects. Multitasking and networking are essential skills for an independent regulatory consultant. Clear and concise communication to different audiences with different backgrounds is a critical skill in a diverse industry.

An independent consultant can contribute at every stage of product development, from strategic planning to the final deliverable, lifecycle management and evaluation. Typically, consultants provide strategic advice to resolve a specific issue or guidance on the development of a product or a certain deliverable, such as the submission of a CE marking application or an orphan designation application.

Listed here are four examples of typical projects for an independent regulatory consultant:

Gap Analysis

To perform a gap analysis, the consultant reviews a project's or product's development status and identifies outstanding items (or "gaps") necessary to move forward toward specific regulatory and/or corporate goals. A gap analysis allows the risks associated with the selected strategy to be identified and evaluated by the development team. With the results of the gap analysis, the client is able to make a better decision on whether to proceed with the selected strategy.

One example of a gap analysis project is reviewing a nonclinical program for a drug and identifying missing studies that are recommended before submission of a clinical trial application. Other examples include a product development assessment for the final preparation in due diligence for a licensing deal or partnership and a quality system evaluation prior to a regulatory agency inspection.

Regulatory Review

During the review of a regulatory submission, such as a clinical trial application (e.g., Investigational New Drug application (IND), Investigational Device Exemption application (IDE)) or registration application (e.g., New Drug Application (NDA), Marketing Authorization Application (MAA), Premarket Approval (PMA), 510k) the consultant ensures that all regulatory requirements for content, structure, format and timelines are met and, if needed, provides comments on how to improve the documents and a list of the potential missing elements.

Very often, the independent regulatory consultant is responsible for writing and assembling the regulatory submission and delivering it to the client for review and comments prior to finalization.

Technical Review

Independent regulatory consultants who have developed considerable expertise in a specific technical area may be asked to provide technical review of a project or application under a specific regulatory framework. For example, a consultant may review the chemistry, manufacturing and controls (CMC) modules of an electronic Common Technical Document (eCTD) NDA or Biologics License Application (BLA) for an innovative drug or biologic or the sterilization or process validation data to support a PMA submission for a medical device. In this case, the consultant primarily will provide comments and suggestions for improvement of the technical content of the reviewed documents.

Project Management

An independent regulatory consultant may be asked to coordinate and provide strategic oversight of a project. In this case, the consultant manages and coordinates the project at the core team level and interacts with all parties involved, potentially including other independent consultants or subcontractors under partnership agreements. The consultant's project management skills may be sought by companies with little experience in regulatory dossier submissions. For instance, a consultant experienced in clinical trial application (CTA) submissions in Europe may provide high-level project management assistance to a US company with no experience in submitting CTAs but with the intention of conducting clinical trials throughout the EU. Likewise, if a company has no experience in managing large projects such as PMAs, NDAs or MAAs, creating and adhering to timelines and identifying rate-limiting steps may be quite challenging and require the services of a consultant.

The remainder of this chapter provides an overview of independent regulatory consulting career aspects, including career timing, defining services, putting systems in place, finding clients, time and money management, maintaining business activity, peaks and troughs in demand and project termination.

Career Timing

Independent regulatory consultants have typically acquired significant field experience in industries such as pharmaceuticals, medical devices, biotechnology, general business consulting or government. They usually specialize in a therapeutic field or product area. Previous professional experience in several settings, either as part of their career path or through collaboration or other activities (e.g., supplier audit) within a single company is helpful in understanding different clients. Direct experience with regulatory authorities (US Food and Drug Administration (FDA), European Medicines Agency (EMA), Notified Bodies) is valuable to prospective clients.

To many regulatory professionals, a career switch from industry to independent consulting presents an attractive option that offers time and workload flexibility and the freedom to take on a project as desired.

Answering the following classic business questions is important when considering independent consulting:
- Do I have a defined business strategy/plan that includes:
  o defined services and core expertise?
  o business development and growth?
- Do I have a comprehensive understanding of my competitors that involves:
  o identification of who they are and how many there are?
  o honest comparison of my assets/weaknesses to theirs?
- Do I have a clear view of potential barriers to enter a chosen market?
- Do I have sufficient professional connections and skills in networking?
- Do I already have potential targets as my first clients with a high likelihood of signing a first contract?

- Do I have a plan to address administrative and legal issues?

References are very important in the specialized field of regulatory affairs. The word of mouth is particularly important in the biotechnology industry where there are fewer actors than in the traditional pharmaceutical sector. Thus, it is essential for an independent regulatory consultant to develop a positive reputation and maintain it throughout his/her career. A solid reputation and network of current and former clients provides the basis for driving the demand for consulting services.

To fully evaluate your readiness to take on the challenges and rewards of independent consulting, it is important to understand the personal qualities and regulatory expertise this field requires, as discussed below.

Personal Attributes of a Successful Consultant
Self-Motivation

As independent regulatory consultants often initially work on their own in a home office, it is important to demonstrate a consistent level of self-motivation. On-site client visits are likely to be the only opportunity to meet face-to-face with other project team members, and may be infrequent if the client is not local. Therefore, contractors usually lack pressure from colleagues to produce on a daily basis.

Self-motivation is particularly important during periods of reduced project activity, when the independent regulatory consultant should ideally focus on business development activities (see "Finding Clients" below).

Efficient Time Management

From before a project's initiation through its completion and regardless of project size, timeline planning is important. Optimizing efficiency to avoid overcharging clients or missing deadlines is highly dependent upon time management skills. Time management is particularly vital when handling several projects in parallel or when working with clients in different time zones or with different milestones. Planning, anticipating, defining priorities and reshuffling as necessary are important qualities of a successful independent regulatory consultant.

Communication and Sense of Diplomacy

Working remotely as a team member on a project magnifies the need for strong communication skills. Client messages that are complex or confusing must be clarified. An independent regulatory consultant must ensure that messages, especially with critical information, are correctly understood and receive follow-up as necessary.

A sense of diplomacy is another valuable quality for an independent regulatory consultant. To a client, the consultant is an external resource who, although integrated in the client team, may not be aware of all underlying internal political issues. The consultant should be diplomatic in conveying an opinion and be prepared in case of disagreement. That said, a major reason why consultants are hired is to provide independent viewpoints, and thus the independent regulatory consultant should not be afraid to present his opinion and recommendations.

Integrity and Confidence

A thorough independent regulatory consultant should explain both the advantages of each potential option and its inherent risks. Integrity and the ability to inspire trust and confidence are valuable attributes that are expected from an independent regulatory consultant who, as an external person, should be less influenced by the client company's hierarchy and organization then the internal staff. However, as discussed in the section above, sensitive matters should be tactfully and clearly brought to the attention of concerned parties to avoid unnecessary conflict or risk having a message misinterpreted.

Openmindedness, Creativity and Flexibility

An independent regulatory consultant should have an open mind and, when appropriate, find creative solutions adapted to each client while bearing in mind that lack of resources may make it difficult for the client to pursue the best path. Creativity is especially important in the early stage of product development, when all available options should be presented to clients. Consultants are expected to have a flexible approach to challenges that come up in projects and remember that not all companies operate in the same way.

Attention to Detail

By definition, independent regulatory consultants must be detail oriented. One responsibility common to regulatory professionals is to ensure that regulatory requirements are applied consistently and carefully throughout the project. Attention to detail is particularly important when regulatory consultants are asked to prepare or review documents for regulatory submissions.

Finding Clients

Identifying potential clients and winning business can be the most challenging aspects of a new career in independent consulting. It is important to be visible within the industry so that the quality of your work can be seen and compared by potential clients. Several approaches to finding and securing a client base are described below.

Activate an Existing Network

An efficient and perhaps obvious approach is to look at the opportunities that your professional network can offer. Independent regulatory consultants who have worked for many years in their industry are likely to have an established network of former employers and colleagues, regulatory contacts, contacts from professional associations, etc. Communicating your availability and services to this network can be a good starting point. However, you should check whether a former contract included a noncompete clause that would preclude working with the organization during a given timeframe. This is a common clause in most employment contracts.

Participate in Seminars and Conferences

Both local seminars and major industry conferences provide valuable opportunities for networking with potential clients and provide a forum to gain visibility by presenting and debating current industry "hot topics" and future developments.

Participate in Professional Organizations

In addition to providing contacts, participation in organizations such as the Regulatory Affairs Professionals Society (RAPS) can give further validity to an independent regulatory consultant's professional status. It may also be helpful to earn a recognized professional certification, such as the Regulatory Affairs Certification (RAC), to enhance your resume. Additionally, publishing articles in your field can expand your name recognition and serve as proof of expertise to potential clients.

Network with Other Independent RA Consultants

Getting to know your competitors may prove useful. Indeed, it is impossible to be an expert in every aspect of regulatory; thus, establishing good relationships with other independent consultants—particularly with complementary expertise—may lead to partnerships or business referrals.

Attend Regulatory Agency Training and Discussions

In addition to expanding your familiarity with leaders in regulatory agencies, training and discussions are important in understanding regulators' concerns and viewpoints. This essential understanding is expected from regulatory consultants. In addition, these meetings offer a good opportunity to meet participants who may be in need of internal regulatory expertise.

Monitor Industry News and Trends

Keeping abreast of current industry trends and breaking news, including financial and product milestones of industry players, can play an important role in all client interactions. This allows you to know when the client may need additional services or flexibility in ongoing activities. It also allows you to identify other potential clients who may need services and gives you an entry point of contact by referring to their breaking news and suggesting how you may help them further advance their programs.

Time Management

When an independent regulatory consultant has several projects to manage simultaneously, task prioritization and reshuffling may be necessary. Before accepting a project, it is important to consider whether quality work can be produced within the client's timelines and the constraints of your current workload. If quality or deadlines could suffer, it is recommended that the consultant discuss the possibility of extending the timeline or reducing the scope of work. If this is not possible, it may be in all parties' best interest to decline this business opportunity or to recommend another consultant from your network to do the job (see "Peaks in Demand" below).

Money Management

Independent regulatory consultants can face a higher risk of unemployment and/or financial difficulties than a consultant employed by a consulting firm. Thus, an independent consultant needs to monitor finances carefully to anticipate any unfavorable trends.

One preventive measure is to research financial reports and filings on a client's website before accepting a new project. If the client is known to be facing a difficult situation, such as limited funding or compliance problems with FDA, an independent regulatory consultant must decide whether to risk working for this organization. However, it can be especially difficult to decline a project in the early stage of the consulting business. If the consultant decides to take the risk of working with a start-up or underfunded client, he or she should carefully monitor the client's financial situation.

It is also critical to have a good accountant and to ensure, to the extent possible, timely payments from clients, e.g., submitting invoices on a schedule and receiving payments in accordance with the agreement. This will ensure that you are being properly compensated and will be able to continue your work with the client as well as support your business.

An independent regulatory consultant also needs to decide whether to charge on an hourly or project basis, and if the latter, how to determine the hourly rate or project fee. Hourly rates will depend upon the market value or scarcity of expertise developed by the independent regulatory consultant—e.g., medical devices development versus drugs or biologics or nonclinical and CMC versus clinical are potential areas of focus—based upon the experience and comfort of the consultant.

In general, strategic decisions regarding money management, such as time spent on billable activities (i.e., client projects) and nonbillable activities (e.g., business development, training/educational activities, etc.) must be carefully considered and made by the independent regulatory consultant.

Putting Systems in Place

The independent regulatory consultant must put information technology (IT) systems and other infrastructure in place to handle project organization, file management, communications, business operations and other activities. These systems should be scalable to accommodate projects of different sizes.

IT (hardware and software) and communication systems (telephone, email and fax) are essential investments that provide the critical, and often only, link to clients. However, an extensive IT system may not be appropriate for an independent consultant due to additional or unexpected maintenance costs. If the business grows to include several consultants, it may be necessary to consider cost-efficient options such as leasing space with IT service available or using contract IT services as needed.

Regulatory and Industry Intelligence

A system or procedure to keep track of regulatory news and industry trends, especially as they relate to existing clients, is a valuable tool. Such a system allows an independent consultant to be rapidly aware of the publication of new information or new regulations and to inform clients quickly.

Developing Quotes for Services and Monitoring Business Activity

Initially, providing an estimate for a proposed service may be a bit difficult. However, after a period of time, statistics on multiple projects can provide a better quantitative and qualitative basis for time and cost estimates. Each project should also be tracked to add experience information to proposals for similar projects. Project data to collect include type of product (drug, biologic, device and indication) and type of project (IND, NDA, etc.), the work that was performed (writing, reviewing, regulatory agency meeting, etc.) and the outcome if known (e.g., approved, allowed, positive, etc.). These statistics can also be a useful marketing tool for gaining similar projects and showing a successful track record.

Defining Services

When defining the services to offer clients, an independent regulatory consultant should identify reasons why a client would ask for his/her assistance rather than engaging a contract research organization (CRO) or consulting firm. Anticipating responses to this question will help build services targeting clients' requirements.

Clients may prefer independent regulatory consultants because:
- they are flexible and responsive
- they are cost-effective
- they can provide specific technical knowledge not commonly found at CROs, e.g., expertise in both science and regulatory affairs
- they can propose more personalized and creative solutions than a large company
- they can be more easily integrated into an existing team

Once services to be offered to potential clients are clearly defined (core expertise), the independent regulatory consultant will be better able to focus on gaining specific clients.

Maintaining Business Activity

Maintaining constant business activity is closely linked to the independent regulatory consultant's ability to satisfy clients, ultimately leading to a solid reputation. Indeed, meeting and exceeding client expectations and gaining client trust are crucial in generating new business. Satisfied clients may serve as references. It is also important to maintain good relationships with clients after projects end to encourage repeat engagements.

Clients expect independent regulatory consultants to be experts in their fields. To meet these expectations, independent regulatory consultants should use a systematic approach to ensure they are continuously acquiring knowledge, keeping skills up-to-date and maintaining a high level of expertise/excellence throughout a project.

Excellence is not only achieved through technical knowledge but also by understanding the different concerns of stakeholders including industry, regulatory agencies, the medical community and patients.

Peaks in Demand

A new independent consulting business can often be challenging financially, but when clients are satisfied by your services and trust your professionalism, work will undoubtedly expand and there may be a time when requests exceed your resources.

There are different ways to handle peaks in demand.

Keep the Business Development Process Simple

Business development activities such as writing proposals and networking or meeting with potential clients can consume a significant amount of your time. Thus, the recommendation is to not overcomplicate the first contacts with potential clients. You may provide a 30-second introduction of yourself and your services (work on refining this to communicate the most important points you want someone to know and remember), provide a brochure with similar details that may be used as a later reference for the potential client, and provide a business card that also lists briefly the services and a website where more information may be found.

Some prospective clients may only contact a consultant to obtain "free" information on a specific topic with no intent of continuing work with the consultant. The relationship must be strategically evaluated to understand what "free" information you can provide and when the client will be required to sign a contract for further consultation.

Stabilize Your Workload Through Selectivity

It is important to accept only projects falling within your defined "core expertise" and to decline those that reach outside your scope. This will allow you to spend your time more efficiently and will ensure that you are providing solid experiential advice as well as maintain your reputation for future business.

In addition, an independent regulatory consultant may choose to prioritize a long-term project over a short-term project because the long-term project will ensure continued work for a period of time, or to choose between a larger company and a smaller company to ensure diversity and balance in stability. However, over-selectivity may kill the business.

Accommodate Activity Increases

Business growth can be accommodated by recruiting administrative support or additional consultants, or by delegating work to external consultants whom you will manage and whose work you will review. The decision to pursue expansion should be based upon your business strategy with regard to growth.

Troughs in Demand

Independent regulatory consultants face periods of decreased business activity due to a number of factors. For example, demand can be reduced when competitors with attractive pricing or services enter the market. Another reason for slowed activity can be changes in regulatory environments, such as a new risk associated with your services. For example, if you assist clients in pharmacovigilance (PV) reporting to agencies and a new regulation increases the responsibilities of the PV reporter, you may decide to cease providing these services.

It is important to try to identify the reasons for a decline in work and take appropriate actions to reverse the trend. Slow demand also should be a signal to brainstorm ways of finding new opportunities and to prioritize business development activities.

Finding New Opportunities

An independent regulatory consultant may choose to pursue new opportunities by adding services. This is a strategic decision that should be carefully considered.

In general, the new services should be complementary to your core expertise and not too different, unless you add new expertise through a partner. For example, if your expertise relates to drug clinical trials submissions and you decide to add consulting services relating to promotion, pricing and reimbursement, potential clients may be puzzled by the lack of connection between these areas and you may lose credibility.

However, partnering with a consultant with different expertise can bring both of you more opportunities through broader service offerings and options for clients. For example, if you are responsible for managing the design control portion of a medical device project but your services do not include technical assistance with sterilization or process validation, you may want to partner with another consultant with that specialty.

If an independent regulatory consultant decides to subcontract some project tasks, it is important to carefully select a provider whose level of quality, timeliness, etc. is on a par with the contractor's. In the end, the independent regulatory consultant is responsible for the quality of the deliverable and the client's satisfaction.

Project Termination

At the beginning of a project, an independent regulatory consultant may have frequent interaction with the company's product development team. However, sometimes this interaction may decrease, leaving the consultant out of strategic discussions and weakening the relationship with the client. This situation can be a source of frustration; the consultant will no longer have the whole picture of the company's goals and concerns, which can affect the quality of strategic advice. Hence, one challenge faced by an independent regulatory consultant is maintaining an ongoing relationship for longer-term projects or for future business and clearly defining the scope of a project for short-term work. The client's needs and goals may also change, causing the client relationship to change as well.

Possible explanations regarding this change in a client relationship are:

Internal Hiring

As the client's company grows, the need for internal regulatory expertise may become unavoidable, such as when product development is progressing or another product is being actively developed in parallel. In this situation, the client's internal regulatory team will eventually take over the independent regulatory consultant's responsibilities. The consultant may offer assistance during the transition.

Client Dissatisfaction

This is the worst-case situation, as once the client develops a negative opinion regarding an independent regulatory consultant's work it is difficult to reverse it. The first thing to do is to identify what went wrong, ideally through direct feedback from the client. If possible, try to correct the problem and regain client confidence. If the client is not responsive or responds negatively to these attempts, the project should be considered over.

Client Financial Constraints

Some clients may face financial difficulties, causing them to slow down development and, potentially, regulatory activities until additional funds have been procured. An independent regulatory consultant may decide to continue performing work for these clients but risks not being paid if capital cannot be raised.

Here is a hypothetical situation: an early start-up asks you to write a regulatory development plan for its product, but only receives funding from government or research grants and is no longer able to pay for your services. After assessing the product's potential and the probability that the company can obtain funding from investors in a later development stage, the independent regulatory consultant may decide to continue collaborating because the future appears positive. Close monitoring of the client's financial situation to the extent possible is essential, however.

Conclusion

Independent regulatory consultants work on projects that can vary considerably in size, budget and duration, depending upon the client's needs and the consultant's expertise and availability. Typical projects include gap analysis, regulatory review of documents for a submission, technical review and project management.

Multitasking, time management, self-motivation, openmindedness, networking, attention to detail and the ability to clearly and concisely communicate are essential skills for an independent regulatory consultant.

A career as an independent consultant may bring great satisfaction, and the transition from employment at a company to an independent business can be done smoothly and naturally.

The process starts by identifying a high level of technical expertise in a particular area likely to be useful to others. Other important factors are a defined business strategy, an understanding of competition, a clear view of potential barriers to entry for a chosen market, sufficient connections and good targets as first potential clients and a plan to address administrative and legal issues.

Once the business is started, information technology and other business infrastructure should progressively be put into place. To acquire clients, "word of mouth" is the best referral system. One of the key goals should be clients' satisfaction, which can help build the consultant's reputation.

As the business grows, selecting clients, managing time and money and maintaining business activity through peaks and troughs in workload become more important. It is also crucial to understand when to terminate a project and how to handle client dissatisfaction if it occurs.

If the business is successful, the consultant will need to decide whether to remain solo or start hiring employees. This decision is not easy and could greatly impact having a successful career of independent regulatory consultant's career.

Acknowledgements
Special thanks to our colleagues: Ingrid Bell, Dr. Stuart Mudge and Kerri-Anne Bowers.

This chapter was inspired by Dr. Emmanuelle Voisin, principal and founder of Voisin Consulting, a firm that assists biotechnology, pharmaceutical and medical device companies in the design and implementation of innovative and global regulatory strategies.

CHAPTER 6

Working as a Self-employed Independent Consultant

By Robert Myers, PhD

Finding Clients

A consulting business is only as strong as its client base. This base can be created in a variety of ways, but creativity and perseverance are essential to success. This chapter will explore how to build a strong and sustainable client base.

Setting up a website and/or advertising in field-related magazines may bring you into contact with companies that would be out of reach any other way. However, these methods have no personal contact and can be costly and somewhat difficult to maintain, especially when just starting a business. A more effective way to contact people is through word of mouth. This is why it is always a good idea to maintain positive connections with your alma mater, the company you left, a former client or your neighbor. Everyone can be a potential contact to grow your business:

- Check in on former co-workers, supervisors and subordinates regularly.
- Locate and inquire about former college associates in your field of expertise.
- Do not be afraid to reacquaint yourself with professors who taught you your trade in the first place. They have a vested interest in your success.
- Pull out all those business cards you collected from the national meetings you attended. Now you know why you saved them.
- Try to attend relevant meetings when possible and financially feasible. Any networking you can do can potentially increase your business. If your

contact person does not have work for you, he or she may know someone who does.

Training and educational courses are another good avenue that will bring you into contact with people in your field. Attendance demonstrates that you are interested in improving your knowledge and skills and allows you to meet others doing the same. This presents the opportunity to meet face-to-face with people who can help you.

Managing Time

As an independent consultant you are self-employed. You're the boss! No one knows when you clock in or clock out. No one watches to see if you come in late or leave early. Only you!

Self-motivation and self-discipline keep an independent consulting business in operation. As an independent consultant, you must produce quality work on time. You must be reasonably available and ready for conference calls or other meetings. If a consultant is consistently late for conference calls or delivering a project, the client may quickly lose trust and respect. It is in your best interest to do what you say you will do when you say you will do it. When a client gets annoyed or unhappy with a consultant, little or no work may be forthcoming.

To complete multiple tasks on time, you must manage time well. If time management is a weakness, you should get training in this area. The bottom line is that time must be spent to keep projects moving along in order to meet deadlines. Calendaring meetings and calls is a great way to be sure nothing slips through the cracks. This is especially true when you are handling multiple projects. Timelines can be set out to track progress to ensure the work is moving at an appropriate pace. The workday may start and end with a quick check of the status of all current projects to be sure you are abreast of your entire workload.

Sticking to an agreed upon timeline is crucial to a consultant's credibility. Since this is so important, you must have clear communication with the client to know what is expected and when. The scope of the work as well as milestones and/or completion dates need to be clearly delineated before the project begins. It is best to have the scope of work and timing in writing to ensure both the consultant and the client agree.

Flexibility in your work schedule can show a willingness to deliver satisfaction and meet the client's needs. Flexibility can be exhibited by working long hours when necessary. When working with clients in other time zones, calls may have to be scheduled outside your normal working hours. Be sure to know the time differences between you and your clients.

Managing Money

An independent consultant is an independent business person. This means that all business dealings are the responsibility of that person. Contracts with clients must be executed to define work to be provided and the payment schedule for the consulting work/project/document. Quotes can be done on a per-piece/project rate or a per-hour rate. When quoting a per-piece/project price, the consultant must be able to accurately estimate the time involved in the preparation of the completed project. The risks in bidding on a per-project basis include underbidding and overbidding. When one underbids, the rate per hour can be diminished to an unacceptable level; if one overbids, the client may look elsewhere for less-expensive services. If the consultant is trying to secure new clients or projects, bids should be on the low side to help land the project and get a foot in the door. To bill on an hourly rate, it helps to ask other consultants or people who work with consultants to determine the fair market rate. Generally speaking, the more experience and expertise the consultant has, the higher the hourly rate can be.

The income that your consulting business produces will need to cover many possible expenses. A salary for yourself as well as any other employees and overhead, such as rent for office space, office equipment, utilities and maintenance, will also need to be paid. These expenses are usually monthly occurrences and are the cost of doing business. Being an independent consultant provides the flexibility to control or minimize many of these costs. You can work at home rather than paying rent for office space. Office equipment and materials can be economized and minimized as needed.

Other expenses may also need to be covered. When one is self-employed, normal benefits usually provided by an employer may need to be purchased. Some of these include medical, dental and/or life insurance. A retirement plan may also be considered. A plan to open individual retirement accounts to systematically save money for retirement is one possibility. Although these expenses may be considered optional, it is wise to be educated and prepared in these areas. Again, you can economize and minimize these expenses by weighing the need versus the cost for each expense. For example, weigh the cost of insurance premiums against the cost of paying expected expenses for the year. Alternatives include flexible spending accounts for medical expenses or just setting aside money rather than paying premiums each month. This is an individual decision and should be made based upon research or the recommendation of a financial advisor.

Another consideration for an independent consultant is that there is no paid time off for vacations, holidays or illness. A consultant gets paid only when working. For these reasons, it is essential to have enough regular or steady work to sustain your business.

Workload can vary from too much to none. To weather these peaks and valleys, you must be able to save in times of plenty for times of "famine." The amount of money to save depends upon monthly expenses and the number of months to be covered.

Tax breaks offer a financial advantage for independent self-employed consultants. Many of the expenses listed above can be written off when filing taxes. The expenses of doing business (equipment, rent, utilities, phone, etc.), certain business vehicles, business losses, medical expenses, insurance premiums, business travel expenses and so forth may be deductible.

On the other hand, there is a financial liability for being an independent, self-employed consultant. This involves the taxes required for this type of business. In the US, these include a self-employment tax (currently 15%) as well as the regular income tax bracket rates. This can easily bring one's tax liability to 40% or more. Without prior planning, this can lead to a hefty tax bill as well as possible penalties from the Internal Revenue Service. Monthly saving and quarterly estimated tax payments can alleviate a large financial burden come 15 April.

Unless the individual consultant is well aware of the current tax laws, it is wise to consult a tax advisor before starting an independent consulting business to be sure what can and cannot be deducted, what receipts should be retained and how taxes should be paid.

Putting Systems in Place

An independent consulting business, like many businesses, must have appropriate systems in place to function properly and smoothly.

There may be many documents to track, most of which will be electronic, and the appropriate hardware and software are needed to handle these electronic files. Although computer files can be backed up on the system, it is advisable to have an external backup as well in the form of an external hard drive, CDs or DVDs. Be sure to label any disks so you can determine what is on them without having to view them. A paper copy of certain key documents can also be kept, but this may not be the most effective way to operate. If a paper copy is desired, a manual filing system will need to be implemented. Electronic and paper files can be organized in a similar fashion. Files can be separated by company, project and portions of a project.

When working on documents, a system should be employed to keep track of the latest version. One can use a base file name with a date and initials and/or version number that can be changed when saving the document (e.g., Section

3.2.P.2.1 v2 17Jan09). When more than one person is working on documents, it is also important to have one person designated as the keeper of the official copies. This person should be the only one who updates the version number of the documents. A record of changes made to a document as well as when and who approves the final document is necessary for a paper trail so the document's history can be traced.

Other systems that should be considered relate to the financial side of the business. If there are employees, a payroll system needs to be in place. On projects that are being billed per hour, a tracking system needs to be established to ensure the correct amount of time is being billed to the client. The billable amounts should be compiled on an invoice for the client. It is wise to have a system to track outstanding and paid invoices. A budget for the business can be helpful in determining where funds are being spent.

Before working with most companies, a contract will need to be signed. The main types are the confidential disclosure agreement (CDA) and the service agreement. Most CDAs are fairly standard documents stating that the consultant cannot disclose any company confidential information. The service agreement contract will usually state what type of work or services will be provided by the consultant, how much the consultant will be paid and when the consultant will be paid. Many times these two contracts are combined into one agreement.

The independent consultant should be aware of any exclusivity agreements or "no compete" clauses. In some contracts, the company will not allow the consultant to disclose that they are working with that particular company. The bottom line here is to read all contacts carefully. If there are portions that are unclear, either talk to a representative of the company or have your own legal counsel review these documents to ensure the company is not asking for anything unreasonable.

One last system to consider is a feedback system. Constructive feedback from a client is a valuable tool to strengthen your business. Continue to do the things that the client likes and improve the things with which the client may not be satisfied. Feedback can be solicited from a client via a phone conversation, email request and/or a simple evaluation form. Although this information is very valuable, it may be difficult to obtain if clients are very busy. It may be necessary to simply ask a client, "Is there anything I can do to be a better consultant for you?"

Building up Services

Although it seems like common sense, be sure to avoid consulting in areas where you have no knowledge. This is not to say that you should not try something new. Just be careful. One of the quickest ways to lose a client is to provide work that is substandard because of ignorance or lack of expertise.

Once you establish a steady client, there may be other areas on which the client requests your expertise. Do your homework and learn the new area as well as you can in order to provide what the client wants. This will help expand the service your business provides.

An alternative approach when a consulting opportunity out of your field of expertise arises is to reach out to your professional network to gain the necessary information. If this type of request keeps coming, you may want to consider bringing people with that particular expertise into your business. This will expand your business capabilities. The expansion of services (employees) needs to be balanced with a steady and secure workload. There have been many consulting businesses that have expanded too quickly only to go out of business due to lack of work to sustain their growth.

Knowing When You Are Ready

The decision to become an independent consultant needs to be based upon several factors. First and foremost, do you have the experience, education and expertise that a client would want? Put yourself in the shoes of a potential client. Would you hire a consultant with only a few years' experience? Would you hire someone with a lack of practical experience in the field? A person must have acquired enough clout in the industry to become a credible consultant.

To be an independent consultant requires clients. Before embarking on a consulting business, it is a good idea to determine how many potential clients you may have and how viable these clients are. This process begins with your personal professional network. Utilizing the guidance in the "Finding Clients" section above, you should be able to draw up a lengthy list of potential clients.

Two more things to consider are whether you are able and willing to work with a flexible schedule and if you have to have the necessary self-motivation and drive that the independent consultant needs to be able to handle the ups and downs (variable workload, income and emotions) of the business. One more factor you will need to think about is where the work will be performed. Is there adequate office space in your primary residence or will an outside office be needed? Space for office equipment and filing systems needs to be available.

Knowing When It Is Over

The decision to end an independent consulting business is not an easy one. This may be more difficult than the decision to become a consultant in the first place. There will be several factors in this decision. If there are no active or potential clients for an extended period, lack of income may force you to end the business. You must weigh your accustomed lifestyle against a decline in income from the business. When your standard of living declines below an acceptable level, it is time to look for other forms of employment—going back to an industry job, joining a larger consulting firm or otherwise changing direction.

CHAPTER 7

Is A Career in a Large, Global Pharmaceutical Company Right for You?

By Bonnie J. Goldmann, MD

When considering regulatory careers at large, global pharmaceutical corporations, it quickly becomes apparent that the only characteristic these corporations have in common (other than expertise in drug discovery and development) is their size. Their structure, culture and decision-making processes, as well as the role and organization of drug development and regulatory, vary considerably. These factors have been further transformed by changes in the economic and political environment that have prompted many companies to reexamine their structures and initiate dramatic reorganizations in order to meet evolving needs.

This chapter provides an approach to thinking about a regulatory career in one of the large, global pharmaceutical companies versus a smaller pharmaceutical or biotechnology company. This approach is not based on theories of organizational design or dynamics, but rather on my own experience "growing up" in a large organization, participating in major reorganizations, leading two large, global regulatory organizations and consulting for companies of various sizes. For each issue, I provide important points to consider as well as specific questions to ask when evaluating a particular job opportunity in a large pharmaceutical company.

Large Versus Small

When evaluating a job opportunity in a large pharmaceutical company, it is important to consider the organization and yourself. This chapter focuses on the organization, but it is critical to know your own strengths, the kind of work environment that works best for you and where you think you can learn and grow. Consider the pros and cons of large versus small (or midsize) companies and the environment that best fits your strengths and needs, depending upon the stage of your career.

The features of large pharmaceutical companies include:

- Availability of a peer group: A larger organization is able to support a reasonably sized peer group whose members have varying degrees of experience from which to learn. In contrast, the number of such peers is necessarily limited in a smaller regulatory organization, in which tasks are contracted out. Although many large companies are now relying more on contract research organizations (CROs), smaller companies rely on CROs to a much greater extent, often contracting out entire processes such as document management. This may limit direct exposure to other regulatory professionals and/or place you in a more managerial role than in a larger company.
- Specialization: In larger organizations there is often specialization within regulatory, with separate groups for labeling; chemistry, manufacturing and controls; compliance; liaison; and policy. In smaller organizations, one person may wear several hats, albeit potentially for fewer products.
- Bureaucracy: There are, by necessity, often more processes and bureaucracy in larger organizations than smaller ones.

Applicants for positions in a larger pharmaceutical company need to understand the following aspects of the organization:

- General organization: location of corporate headquarters, centralized versus decentralized governance, geographic versus therapeutic focus or matrix
- Product lifecycle management: product development, decision processes, lifecycle management
- Regulatory organization: role in product lifecycle management, specialization, regional versus global versus therapeutic focus, approach to and reputation with regulatory agencies

General Organization

Large, global pharmaceutical companies can be US companies or non-US companies. Although in and of itself this may not seem important, it may have certain pragmatic implications worth considering. Specifically, it is important to understand whether the company views itself as a US company with a global presence or an international company with a US presence. Many US companies with a global presence function in a very US-centric way with a focus primarily on US Food and Drug Administration (FDA) requirements. In contrast, many non-US companies have a very different perspective, which may result in one regional regulatory group being perceived as a "second sister" to the others.

Another aspect to consider is the location of the corporate headquarters. If you are located in the US and the corporate headquarters is in Europe, a great deal of travel may be required. Further, in some companies, it is important to have work experience at the corporate headquarters in order to advance past a certain level. This may necessitate relocating, possibly to another country, to further your career.

Before joining any company, it is important to consider corporate governance (which has implications for decision making and resource allocation as well as the potential degree of bureaucracy). Is the company centralized or decentralized? Are decisions made at the lower levels with review and ratification at a more senior level, or are proposals made to the senior level for a decision? Who participates in decision making? Is a broad group of people directly involved in product development or just the more senior members of the team?

In addition, is the company organized by specific therapeutic areas or specific geographic regions? This is often more than just a matter of emphasis and may have implications for reporting relationships, decision making and the structure of functional groups such as regulatory. It is important to completely understand these organizational relationships, especially as they relate to reporting, so that it is clear whether you are becoming part of a broad regulatory organization, a regulatory organization within a therapeutic area or a regulatory organization within a regional organization. In this context it is also important to understand whether there are dual reporting relationships and, if so, at what level(s) of the organization. This information can be obtained by looking at organizational charts published on a company's website, if available, or by asking these relevant questions during the interview process.

Product Lifecycle Management

Product lifecycle management often focuses on the postapproval phase. For our purposes, however, true lifecycle management extends from discovery to patent expiration. There are several different ways companies manage the various phases of drug development. In certain cases, work on each phase of development—discovery, early development (clinical pharmacology and nonclinical pharmacology and toxicology), late development (Phase 2 and 3) and postapproval—is separate with multiple hand-offs. More often than not, however, there is at least a continuum between early and late development.

How a particular company approaches lifecycle development and management and the role of regulatory in this process are key in deciding whether the company is a good fit. Ideally, regulatory is involved in all phases of development (but certainly prior to consideration of first-in-human studies). If each phase of development is handled separately, will you have the opportunity to be involved in different phases over time? Each phase presents a different set of questions and decisions and requires different problem-solving approaches and agency interactions. Breadth of experience is important in developing as a regulatory professional. For example, are there opportunities prior to New Drug Application (NDA) submission for regulatory to chair the project team? Understanding the opportunities or limitations for regulatory professionals during the entire product lifecycle should thus be a key determinant in deciding on a job with the company.

Regulatory Organization Within the Company

Consideration of the organization of the regulatory department within a large pharmaceutical company should focus on several broad categories:
- Organizational structure of the department: regional or therapeutic, specialized functions
- Functional role within the company: in product lifecycle, on product development teams, and in overall decision making
- Agency relationships
- Growth opportunities

Organizational Structure

A global regulatory department can be organized by region, e.g., US or North America, EU, Japan, emerging markets; by therapeutic area, e.g., neurology, endocrinology; or by both in a matrix structure. More than many other functional groups, regulatory requires geographic expertise as well as expertise in a specific therapeutic area. Because functions such as clinical are usually organized by therapeutic area, it is natural to want to organize regulatory similarly, especially since product development often takes place within therapeutic areas. However, understanding regulatory perspectives and requirements in different geographic regions is essential to global approval of a product. Several organizations have created a matrix with both regional and therapeutic regulatory groups and dual reporting relationships to accommodate the need for both types of expertise.

Regulatory is not simply one function; it requires expertise based upon specific competencies and knowledge in areas such as liaison with agencies, product labeling, chemistry and manufacturing, document management and policy. At one end of the spectrum is a department in which one person is expected to provide all the regulatory functions for a specific product, which is not generally the model in larger companies. At the other is a department with a separate group for each specific function. Within those extremes are variations or combinations of functions. Additionally, some companies separate early product development from late product development. Questions to ask when assessing how the regulatory department is organized include: How many products is one person expected to manage in the context of specialization? Is there a team approach that encourages sharing of information and expertise for learning across different areas of expertise? Is there opportunity to move from one area of expertise to another?

Functional Role in the Organization

Regulatory can be perceived and valued in several different ways within an organization: as a key partner in the development of products, as an important negotiator with global agencies, as guardian of compliance with regulations or a group that ensures that information is in the correct form for agencies. In determining regulatory's role and how it is perceived within the organization, it is helpful to explore the following questions:
- What is the role the group plays in the product lifecycle?
    As noted above, knowing regulatory's degree of involvement in the different phases of the product lifecycle is important. Is regulatory a major contributor and decision maker within the development team or relegated to taking direction and implementing the team's decisions?
- Are the members of regulatory part of decision making at all levels of the organization, such as within the product teams and governance/decision-making committees?
    Is the regulatory organization freestanding or a section of another group such as clinical development or marketing? Are the leaders of regulatory key to the company's decision making on broader development or governance issues?

Agency Relationships

Prior to joining a company, it is essential to understand its philosophy and approach regarding various global agencies, as well as its reputation with those agencies. Does the company work with agencies in a partnership? Is the company aggressive? What are the agencies' perceptions of the company? Since you will likely be working directly with the agencies, their perception of the company will most likely influence their perception of you. This information can be obtained during the interview process where you can ask about company philosophies; you can also find some information by looking at the FDA website for Warning Letters and approvals to determine the obligations and relationships with FDA. Similarly, you can search the EMA website for interactions that may provide some insight into the perceptions held by that agency about the company.

Evaluating the company's general approach and attitude is important since you will be expected to deliver results within that context. Determine whether the company understands the importance of "regulatory as negotiator" and its role in finding common ground and mutually agreeable solutions, or whether the company perceives regulatory as simply representing agency positions and, therefore, part of the "problem." Much of the negotiating done by regulatory personnel occurs within their own companies, so understanding how regulatory is perceived by colleagues is critical.

Growth Opportunities

It is important to consider possibilities for growth within the regulatory organization as well as the company as a whole. This can be determined by evaluating the structure of the department and the flexibility given to personnel in performing different functions, as well as the department's commitment to training, the existence of clearly defined job descriptions, the definition of required competencies, and the availability of mentoring. It is helpful to try to judge the organization's stability and the ability of successful members to advance within the company both within and outside regulatory. Have members of the department been able to take leadership roles in other organizations within the company? Have they participated in special assignments or chaired cross-functional committees? What are the characteristics and skills of those who have been successful in the regulatory organization? The answers to these questions will help determine both how the department is regarded within the larger organization as well as the potential for career growth.

Information Gathering

As you go through the job application process, do not hesitate to ask questions such as those presented in this chapter. Take the opportunity to talk with people you know in the corporation, even from areas outside regulatory. Search the company's website and review its annual report. Review the organizational charts of the regulatory organization as well as the decision-making committees and process. Be sure to review the information in the public domain about recent global submissions and regulatory actions. All this information needs to be assessed in the context of where you are in your career development, the type of organization you want to be a part of, and where you think you can be successful.

Conclusion

Being part of a regulatory organization in a large, global corporation can be challenging and rewarding. However, to ensure a successful regulatory career at a large company, it is important to understand the overall organization, its philosophical and tactical approach to product development, and the part regulatory plays. Applying this knowledge in the context of your own strengths, skills and comfort with different types of organizational structures should help to ensure a rewarding career.

CHAPTER 8

Working in a Large Pharmaceutical Company

By Paul Gil, PhD, RAC

The best thing about working in the regulatory department of a large pharmaceutical company is the unique career and learning opportunities that it offers. In a large company, many colleagues have different experiences and backgrounds to support a wide variety of projects. Information and learning are often available from local sources instead of external contacts at regulatory agencies and other companies. This allows an individual to be exposed to many different perspectives and find experienced mentors.

In a small company, there are usually more opportunities to interface with top management and potentially shape the organization. In a large organization, impact is more often made through teams as opposed to individual efforts. Closer professional relationships may result from this teamwork.

Before pursuing a career at a large pharmaceutical company, regulatory professionals should be aware of three myths.

The Three Myths
1. **More resources are available in a large pharmaceutical company.**

Large pharmaceutical companies may have larger headcounts and much more depth in expertise, but they do not necessarily have more available resources. More personnel do not automatically translate into "available" personnel and, because there are additional products and activities, resource allocation is typically just as tight as in a smaller company. The industry is facing intense market pressures to find new, innovative drugs to replace existing ones as patents expire. Escalating research costs coupled with scientific challenges and increased regulatory hurdles all contribute to the pressure. Within the large organization, levels of activity demanding resources may vary tremendously, depending upon factors such as the number of products in the pipeline, new products and facilities being licensed and postapproval changes.

2. Large pharmaceutical organizations have a widely shared knowledge base.

Sharing of knowledge does not occur unless communication is effective. Successful organizations incorporate adaptability, responsiveness and openness in communication into a changing environment. In large pharmaceutical organizations, there can be tremendous barriers to communication, including multiple branches/divisions, bureaucracy and turf wars. The use of databases and team rooms can facilitate the exchange of tremendous amounts of complex information. Regulatory must capture and analyze data from patients, clinical, manufacturing, Quality Assurance (QA), quality control (QC) and others.

Further, knowledge acquisition, creation and sharing are dependent upon the information technology system. Organizations must process huge amounts of data from their dynamic environments and be responsive and adaptable to maintain competitive advantage. Continual updates to reduce the need for information processing or increase the capacity of the information processing system are needed. In response to this trend, many large pharmaceutical organizations have implemented new surveillance systems and increased lateral connections internally.

3. A large pharmaceutical company offers fewer opportunities to handle multiple roles and wider responsibilities.

Since smaller companies have many roles that need to be filled by only a few people, there are many opportunities to assume broad responsibilities in key areas. But larger organizations, under competitive pressures to do more with less, create similar opportunities for high-visibility roles with enormous impact. For example, in some large, multinational pharmaceutical companies, regulatory strategists have worldwide responsibilities for all regulatory aspects of a product throughout the lifecycle. In a large company, there are diverse projects, such as assessment of new potential projects or assessment of options for a product's lifecycle, in which the regulatory professional can become a leader or active participant—many with the potential for huge impact and financial savings.

Polish Skills

Rewards and recognition for excelling in the above-mentioned roles and responsibilities typically emphasize a common set of skills. Communication skills always appear at the top of the list and encompass both internal and external contacts. Highly competent written and verbal communication skills, including technical writing, are prerequisites for any regulatory job, regardless of the environment, but it is especially important in a large company to break down the barriers that make communication challenging. In regulatory, understanding agency expectations and addressing agency requirements are paramount. Conveying information in a clear and succinct manner to regulatory agencies is an essential part of gaining approvals. Knowing what to present and how to present it in the most direct manner will increase chances of single-cycle reviews. Agency personnel tend to be overworked, so verbal and written contacts must be succinct and to the point. Respect for regulators' time goes a long way. Presenting a structured outline with only the pertinent data will enable a more focused review. The same approach applies to agency meetings. Well-organized and rehearsed presentations will alleviate confusion and expedite the approval process. Regulatory professionals have the responsibility of optimizing the meeting presentation to ensure it is on target and efficient.

Gone are the days when regulatory professionals simply wrote submission cover letters. Today's trend is to increase one's professional value by being knowledgeable about the science behind the clinical and chemistry, manufacturing and controls (CMC) aspects. Understanding the technical issues and solving problems are essential skills. Regulatory professionals must be able to think logically and offer strong, clear, scientific rationales to defend challenges to company positions. It is inefficient and frustrating for a reviewer who calls regulatory with a simple technical question to find the regulatory person is not technically versed and is unfamiliar with the submission. A call with subject matter experts from within the organization at a later date may be required for complex issues; however, the majority of clarification questions can and should be answered by the regulatory respondent during the initial contact. In addition to annoyance, delays in answers may lead to an incomplete review letter and a second-cycle review because reviewers have waited to inquire until late in the review cycle timeline.

Regulatory professionals also must have expertise in science and strategy to provide sound regulatory advice to internal teams. This requires technical understanding of the clinical process for early drug development, the manufacturing process and reporting requirements for postapproval changes, just to mention a few areas. Regulatory professionals are challenged to synthesize and interpret large amounts of data from many areas to create reasoned and rational strategies to guide the organization.

Nurturing relationships and building a good reputation with colleagues, agency reviewers and agency inspectors are skills that rarely get enough attention. Honesty and trust go a long way in any work environment. Being sensitive to the needs and interests of others, openly acknowledging their contributions, fostering a collaborative environment and being socially adept are essential to success.

Transform Interactions Into Collaborations

Regulatory professionals in large organizations rarely work alone on projects. In a large organization, they interact with a diverse group of individuals from many disciplines, including research and development, clinical, operations, marketing, QA and QC. It is important to realize that every interaction presents the opportunity for a collaborative relationship. These relationships promote informal networks that facilitate knowledge flow. Collaborations are crucial to organizational effectiveness and competitive success in today's fast-changing and highly competitive knowledge-based industries. Also, cross-functional teams whose members communicate, share information, and work together in and outside their respective discipline with few boundaries serve as an organization's most effective problem-solving mechanism.

Become a Regulatory Leader

To create the force that captures the imagination and empowers the team, regulatory leaders must structure work in ways that are mind-enriching, heart-fulfilling, soul-satisfying, and financially rewarding. For a regulatory team leader to create an atmosphere of trust and actively foster collaboration, consider a five-step action plan.

Step 1. Share Experiences and Connect Emotionally

The first step is to share regulatory experiences with other regulatory professionals in your company and build trust with colleagues in the work environment—within both regulatory functions and project teams. If a team is seeking advice about a particular regulatory strategy, be open and honest. Discuss realistic timelines and expectations and be prepared to present alternatives. A focus on the feelings and perceptions that are beneath the words of others will help to establish an emotional connection and evoke a sense of trust.

Step 2. Resist Impulses and Suspend Judgments

Regulatory professionals should strive for high self-awareness and a control of their emotions and feelings to create an environment of trust and fairness. Self-awareness is associated with self-control, even temper, predictability, restraint, calm and trustworthiness. By suspending judgments, seeking out information, and mastering their emotions, leaders are able to adapt to changes and build integrity. For example, during an inspection, a regulatory agency investigator may interpret data differently than the company did. A good regulatory leader perceives and manages negative emotions such as frustration and disappointment. Regulatory should set the example and focus the team to think critically, deconstruct problems, and reach unemotional conclusions rather than becoming flustered or angry and mishandling the situation.

Step 3. Empower and Motivate Others

Learning is the foundation of effective leadership. A regulatory leader who continually develops employees will help ensure organizational success. Large pharmaceutical companies tend to have more funds available for training and development, technical seminars and symposia. Seize this opportunity. Also, invite your staff to lead projects and teach and mentor them along the way.

Motivated leaders have a passion to go beyond the minimum requirements and are driven by the desire to achieve. Communication is a key element in the leader's ability to motivate others. Complacency causes poor performance and sustained motivation requires periodic renewal. Continually tracking results and offering motivation to reach goals and objectives will maintain or increase optimism and commitment to the organization and allow for new challenges to be accepted.

Empowering others involves letting go and giving power away. As a leader develops and advances within the organization, successors need to be in place to fill the vacancy. Give employees the opportunity to exercise leadership and boost their confidence to tackle tough challenges. Train your successor.

Step 4. Listen Carefully With Focused, Genuine Interest

In large pharmaceutical organizations, formal systems, layers of bureaucracy and barriers may slow or inhibit communication. Regulatory leaders should turn away from organizational positions and politics toward attentiveness and genuine concern for others. Empathetic leaders sense the viewpoints of others and consider employees' feelings and other factors when making decisions. Work closely with your colleagues and listen to them. They may have concerns about data, a particular submission or global strategy. Listening with empathy shows genuine concern. Hearing others' perspectives and different experiences shows support and boosts their self-esteem. Showing genuine interest and enthusiasm builds employee morale and commitment. Practice listening skills and focus on the emotional makeup of others to enhance empathy. Mentoring can also build closer relationships that lead to empathy.

Step 5. Network and Recognize the Contributions of Others

Social skills play a role in influence, communication, conflict management, leadership, change, bond building, collaboration and cooperation and team capabilities. Social skills help you manage relationships with others. In a large company, regulatory leaders can use social skills to encourage networking and persuade others to cooperate and deliver on commitments. Interact frequently and build relationships and rapport widely across the organization to enhance social skills. The key to successful organizational leadership centers on being sensitive to others. Having good personal relationships helps to build an environment of trust. Listening, focusing, and being attentive to the environment surrounding business interactions helps individuals connect.

Large organizations usually have many lucrative and creative means to reward and recognize others. Personally delivering recognition and rewards also shows respect and gratitude and helps solidify relationships.

Be Effective in Large Organizations

The pharmaceutical industry has evolved from a relatively stable structure dominated by large, vertically integrated firms and an innovative, but maturing, technological environment to a large base of small pharmaceutical and biotechnology companies, which has created great potential for new economic activities and induced important changes. The power of larger organizations lies within their ability to utilize the knowledge and diversity of each individual within the organization. Databases and team rooms facilitate the collection and exchange of information. Working together and frequently exchanging data, information and knowledge leads to cost savings, process optimization and better decision making than any one individual could probably achieve on his or her own.

Effectiveness within large pharmaceutical organizations is highly influenced by collaborative relationships and interpersonal interactions. A collaborative climate is one of the major factors influencing effectiveness and organizations need to promote teamwork in a collaborative atmosphere where information is freely exchanged, differences in opinions and values are shared, and trust is established. Effective organizational leadership is a dialog through which leaders identify and communicate with their constituents to share knowledge and find meaning. Because the involvement of regulatory professionals transcends the product lifecycle, network and leadership opportunities are abundant. By building relationships, mentoring and collaborating, regulatory plays a key role sharing values, gaining understanding and expressing our organization's culture.

Stay Aware of Changes in Regulations and Be Adaptive

Global competition and changes in the economy in recent years have forced organizations to become more flexible and manage change more effectively. Regulatory professionals must stay current with the changing regulatory agency climate, guidance and laws. Interpreting regulations, using tools such as comparability protocols to reduce reporting requirements, and providing sound strategic advice on regulatory strategies can be key aspects of competitive advantage.

Business deals such as mergers and acquisitions (M&As) can change an organization's focus, strategy, staff, systems and even the culture itself. Managers in the global pharmaceutical industry need to be aware that organizational upheavals such as those brought about by M&As and restructuring will impact their level of stress and mental health. During such restructuring, uncertainty and lack of communication often cause the greatest stress. Organizational leaders, including those in regulatory, must adjust and adapt their style to the new environment and help their people through it.

Choosing the Right Regulatory Career

Chapter 9

Small Company Perspective

By Meredith Brown-Tuttle, RAC

A small company is in the eye of the beholder. From my perspective, a small company might have 10 people and a large company 1,000 employees, while a person from a large biotech of 30,000+ people would think "small" means one fewer than 3,000 people. The size of a small company will often dictate the number of people in the regulatory department and their skill levels.

Small Company Environment

Chaotic, hectic, disorganized, creative, fun, flexible and thriving are just a few ways to describe what you will find behind the doors of a small company. To thrive in a small company you need to be comfortable with ambiguity and tasks that you have not necessarily done before. An ability to deal with a lack of infrastructure or to create one with few resources is helpful.

Regulatory Skills Needed to Thrive in a Small Company

Just as a small company needs a kaleidoscope of talent to make it prosper, the regulatory professional needs a solid skill set to do well. These skills include but are not limited to:
- good written and verbal communication, oral presentation and organizational skills
- background in clinical, nonclinical, manufacturing or any combination
- able to multi-task and work on multiple global projects

- good computer skills in Microsoft Word and Adobe Acrobat, at a minimum, for publishing submissions
- curiosity and the ability to look at many types of documents for submission and ask questions and follow up with research if needed
- ability to do quality assurance, pay attention to detail and review documents for consistency and errors
- analytical skills to understand the impact of guidance documents, regulations and other requirements on the company and the discipline to keep up on regulatory precedents
- fearlessness: the courage to do something you have never done before
- ability to get along well with others and understand a variety of perspectives or be very creative in dealing with a variety of challenging personalities
- ability to deal with a constantly changing environment
- resourcefulness: figuring out how to do the same job that large companies perform with more people and tools
- holistic view of drug development and of a particular submission to break down the components for the team and set goals
- networking skills: with fewer resources, you will need to depend upon your "external" regulatory network to answer questions or provide information
- creativity to manage with less and find solutions without a lot of resources; creativity also helps when cutting and pasting documents from many different formats into one submission
- negotiating skills to achieve compromise within the team without causing animosity

Organizational Considerations

No matter how small or large a company, the regulatory department always needs two things: a visionary leader who has extensive regulatory experience and can plan strategy and one or more subordinates to implement the vision and produce the submissions. **Table 9-1** characterizes the mix of leadership and staff you might find at a small company, based on size.

The number of regulatory staff is dictated by the volume of products that are approved or in development and the level of support needed.

Table 9-2 provides a general view of each level's responsibilities, although in a small company these lines may blur and overlap.

Table 9-1. Small Company Staff and Leadership

Company Size	Leadership	Subordinates by Level
Fewer than 10 people	Vice president, senior director or director (usually only one or the other)	Usually a vice president or director must handle both strategy and tactics, or hire a consultant to produce submissions
10-30	Vice president, senior director or director (usually only one or the other)	Regulatory associate or manager
30-100	Vice president, senior director or director (usually only one or the other)	Regulatory associate or manager Regulatory publisher or administrative person
100-200	Vice president, senior director or director (usually only one or the other)	Regulatory manager Regulatory associate or senior associate Regulatory publisher
200-300	Vice president, senior director or director (usually only one or the other)	Regulatory manager Senior regulatory associate Regulatory associate Regulatory publisher (one or two)
300-500	Vice president	Director or senior director Regulatory manager (one or two) Senior regulatory associate Regulatory associate (one or two) Regulatory publisher (one or two)
500-1000	Vice president or senior vice president	Director or senior director Associate director Regulatory manager (one or two) Senior regulatory associate Regulatory associate (one or two) Regulatory publisher (two or more)

Qualifications, Knowledge, Skills and Abilities
Degree Discrimination

There are many talented regulatory professionals with many years of experience on the job, but no formal four-year degree. These individuals are often discriminated against when they try to find a job, even at a small company. Small companies need to make every staff member's talents and qualifications count, and therefore look for the best resume—including a bachelor's degree. Bachelor of science degrees are preferred, but there are also those with bachelor of arts degrees who have learned all the appropriate medical terminology; it really depends upon the person and his or her willingness to learn the profession.

TABLE 9-2. REGULATORY STAFF POSITIONS, RESPONSIBILITIES AND SKILLS

Job Function/Level	Responsibilities and Skills
Vice president/ Senior vice president	<ul><li>Business operations (budgeting, hiring, interacting with the executive team)</li><li>Regulatory strategy, including overseeing all types of major regulatory filings (IND, CTA, NDA, MAA)</li><li>Relationships with regulatory agencies, including style of communication and submissions</li><li>Typically has an advanced degree (MS, JD, PhD, MD)</li><li>Must have leadership and management skills as well as the technical skills of lower level positions</li><li>"Senior" position will have more years of experience</li></ul>
Director/Senior director	<ul><li>Regulatory strategy, including global regulatory strategy</li><li>Hiring and evaluation of employees and consultants</li><li>Regulatory intelligence</li><li>Run regulatory team meetings and/or part of development team</li><li>Lead large regulatory filings</li><li>Review submissions written by other team members</li><li>Could lead the department</li><li>"Senior" position will have more years of experience</li></ul>
Associate director	<ul><li>Same duties as senior manager</li><li>Implement regulatory strategy</li><li>Conduct regulatory intelligence</li><li>Respond to agency requests for information</li></ul>
Senior manager	<ul><li>Same duties as manager</li><li>Learn regulatory strategy</li><li>Organize larger submissions, such as NDAs, MAA</li></ul>
Manager	<ul><li>Starts conducting regulatory intelligence</li><li>Researches, writes, and organizes submissions</li><li>Oversees submission publishing process</li><li>Conducts team interactions</li><li>Mentors associates</li></ul>
Senior associate	<ul><li>Same as associate level duties</li><li>Start filling in on team meetings as a back-up to manager</li><li>Learn how to research, organize and write submissions</li></ul>

Job Function/Level	Responsibilities and Skills
Associate	• Anything that is assigned by the regulatory manager/director/vice president • Learn how to coordinate and write and submit annual reports, IND safety reports and investigator submissions • Write FOI requests • Review all investigators on the disqualification and debarment list • Reading and learning the code of federal regulations and appropriate guidance documents • Help with publishing of submissions including formatting and creates and updates submission chronology
Technical publisher	• Performs copy editing • Formats all documents according to a style guide • Creates documents for electronic publishing, such as hyperlinking, bookmarking, etc. • Copy/print and assemble submissions • Creates and updates submission chronology

Individuals with MDs or PhDs may be hired at the manager or director level; however this may be a disadvantage as they tend not to learn the "ropes" of the job and these gaps in their knowledge can affect their management skills.

Attitude

Those who thrive and survive in a small company are a special breed who love change and the creative challenges of limited resources. Many individuals accustomed to large organizations have tried and failed to transition to a smaller company. Those who have adapted have found a whole new world of knowledge and enriching experiences.

Adaptation at a small company requires a flexible mindset and a willingness to do just about anything that is needed—from writing a submission or the investigator's brochure to helping with shipping and receiving, replacing paper in the printer, or making copies.

Transitioning From a Large Company to a Small Company

"Adapt or die" and "Think of all the opportunities to learn" are the mottos you need to carry with you when you take a position at a small company after spending all or most of your career at a large company. First, you will experience culture shock because the company you came from is probably radically different from the one you have joined. Second, you will learn that one person or only a few people represent a department, unlike where you came from and that you will have to adapt to having fewer resources and a heavier individual workload. Third, given the limited resources across the company, you will have an opportunity to perform a broader scope of work and activities than in larger companies.

Tips to Help the Transition
- Expect things to be different, sometimes very different, from your previous company.
- Expect your job responsibilities to be different and probably broader, rather than as deep, as before.
- Instead of saying, "That's how we did it at 'Big Company X,'" which can alienate your peers and teammates, rather, find out how the small company has done things in the past and make careful suggestions without citing the company name.
- Anticipate a big change and allow six months to make the adjustment.
- Do not expect to be able to delegate a task; you probably will have to do it yourself, so learn how.
- Do not expect the same resources or tools that you used to have; you will need to be creative.
- Do not expect to come in at 9:00 and leave at 5:00—you will need to stay until the work gets done, even if it interferes with your home life.
- The timeline for a small company is more compact and deadlines are tighter than at large firms with the money to bring in outside consultants or multiple layers of management approval.
- If an idea works, it will often be approved at the same meeting and the team will expect you to act on it.
- A department usually consists of only one to three people.
- Project management is not always delegated to a specific person; it may be a shared function.

Moving up the Ladder: How to Advance
How quickly you advance at a small company depends upon:
- opportunities to learn new skills
- your motivation to learn new skills and take on responsibilities
- the stage of development of the company's compounds/products
- corporate growth or potential for growth

Small Company Perspective

TABLE 9-3. SAMPLE PARADIGM OF REGULATORY ADVANCEMENT

Job Function/ Level	Promotion To	Years on Job Before Advancement to Next Level
Senior director	Vice president	2–5 or indefinitely+
Director	Senior director	2–4
Associate director	Director	1–2
Senior manager	Associate director*	2–3
Manager	Senior manager	2–3
Senior associate	Manager	1–2
Associate	Senior associate	1–2

*This tends to be the hardest transition from manager/senior manager to director level and then again from director to vice president, which is considered an officer of the company.
+Some professionals get stuck at this level and never move up to vice president.

People pick up and master skills at different rates. Increases in skills, knowledge and experience usually determine how often and when promotions come. Another factor is upward mobility. If everyone is happy and no one leaves, if the company downsizes or if it does not expand due to financial constraints, promotions may be hard to win.

Small company advancement is generally less competitive than in larger companies because there are fewer individuals eligible for an open position. Advancement is based upon merit and availability of the position. Although there is no firm rule in the amount of time required before advancement, **Table 9-3** shows an approximate length of time one might expect to remain in a position prior to being promoted.

Job Titles at a Small Company

If you take a job at a smaller company, your new job title will often be more impressive than the title you left with the large company. This occurs because smaller companies, which may not be able to provide the same salary and perks as a large company, try to compensate with a promotion—at least on paper. Also, smaller companies with fewer management layers have greater flexibility to elevate titles.

Finding Your First Job in Regulatory

When you first graduate from college or enter the pharmaceutical industry, you will probably have an idea of the job you would like to perform, but that initial job may be quite different from your ultimate career focus. A small company is ideal for your first job. Working in a small pharmaceutical company often will allow you to experiment with different job functions, including clinical research, data management, regulatory, administrative, project management and manufacturing, because you can help out as needed, learning a bit about the job function as you do it. This gives you the opportunity to find your place in the pharmaceutical industry without jumping from company to company.

Breaking into the pharmaceutical industry can be difficult and requires perseverance, so the best strategy is to take a position wherever you can get one, in a large or small company, and acquire experience that can lead to other jobs. The only problem is that some small companies will not hire people unless they have extensive experience because they want the person to "hit the ground running" with little oversight and direction.

Transitioning Into Regulatory

Working in a small company, you are in a good position to transition into regulatory. How do you do this? First, wait until you can handle the work in your current job. Then, at the water cooler or in the lunchroom, start a conversation with members of the regulatory department to find out more about what they do, what their daily activities are and what they like or dislike about their jobs. Invite a regulatory person to lunch for an in-depth conversation. Then, you can express interest in helping out on the next big project. In small companies, "cross-training" is both encouraged and needed as there are limited resources. This will help get you exposure with the regulatory department. As regulatory team members come to rely upon and expect your help, you will be their first thought on how to fill the opening when the department expands or someone leaves. Coupled with a certificate or master's degree in regulatory to provide the necessary background, that is a strategy for breaking into regulatory.

What You Can Do to Help the Transition to Regulatory

The following additions to your resume can encourage others to see your potential for a regulatory position and give you a chance to make the transition.
- writing samples (abstracts, journal articles, course assignments)
- demonstrated skills in project management and organization
- demonstrated willingness to put in the time to learn and to learn in a variety of areas
- regulatory education courses, such as those offered at University of California, Santa Cruz

Small Company Perspective

Advantages of Small Companies
- exposure to a wide variety of tasks versus working in a "silo" as you would in a large company
- faster professional growth and skills acquisition because you are exposed to more variety, challenges and issues
- your job responsibilities can overlap other functions and levels, allowing you to gain more experience
- ability to explore a new career by volunteering to help out in another department
- with fewer layers of management, decisions are made and strategy set quickly
- opportunity to make a difference, not just act as another "cog" in the wheel
- participation in building infrastructure provides a learning experience

Disadvantages of Small Companies
- no defined or formal training program—all of it is on the job—and critical parts of the training might be missing (which you only find out if you go to another company)
- expectation that you will hit the ground running and have a variety of existing skills; if you do not have the skills, money and/or time for training are usually not available
- standard operating procedures (SOPs) are often not in place and need to be written
- fast pace and frequent changes in strategy lead to "loose ends" that never get finished
- lack of resources to complete critical tasks
- heavy reliance on consultants, whose opinion may be valued more than employees'
- fewer professional peers to validate ideas unless you have an outside network of colleagues
- small size can mean everyone knows everybody else's business

Chapter 10

Working at a Small Pharmaceutical Company

By Scott Oglesby, PhD

Say you have just joined (or are considering joining) a small pharmaceutical company in a regulatory position. There is a good chance that the company is funded by venture capital (or even angel investors) and has yet to develop a revenue stream, and you are either the only regulatory person or part of a very small group.

When I joined my first small pharmaceutical company, it had just completed yet another round of financing and was getting ready to prepare its first Investigational New Drug (IND) application and conduct clinical trials in the US. Looking back, I realize now that a number of organizational considerations had an impact on the regulatory role.

The regulatory group or individual should report directly to the CEO because regulatory entails legal corporate responsibilities and accountability, especially when managing an active IND. This structure ensures that regulatory is involved in executive meetings, able to make senior management aware of legal and regulatory responsibilities, and in a position to propose regulatory strategies and obtain adequate resources.

Generally, regulatory emerges within a small company as the company moves toward submitting its first IND in the US or similar first-time submission in another region. As the regulatory activities pick up, the challenge is whether to use internal resources (if already established), hire additional resources or contract out the needed activities. The scenario will be different for each company depending upon size, maturity and anticipation of ongoing activities. I believe small companies should define their core competencies and strategically important core activities early and ensure they are performed by company staff and not contracted out.

For example, at the first start-up company I worked for, we decided that clinical protocols and clinical study reports were strategically important to the company in accurately and consistently evolving the story for our products. We therefore developed protocol and clinical study report templates. For protocols, we obtained outside input into technical and logistical aspects of study designs, but wrote protocol synopses and full protocols ourselves. For clinical study reports, we contracted out data management and statistical services, but took the data and wrote the clinical study reports ourselves. To manage the work that was contracted out, a project coordinator was hired to help develop templates, track documents and review cycles and interface with outside contract groups, including those involved in preparing our documents for submission to regulatory agencies.

The resources required to keep track of and manage multiple outside vendors can rapidly escalate. If possible, companies should consider contracting with only a few groups and letting them provide the first layer of project management.

Finally, even for small pharmaceutical companies, drug development today is a global activity. Therefore, it is important to choose vendors with the on-site staff and expertise in key regions that are important for development of your product(s). These vendors can provide knowledge of regional regulatory requirements and act as your company's local regulatory agent when required.

Qualifications, Knowledge, Skills and Abilities

Table 10-1 highlights important attributes for different levels of responsibility in a small pharmaceutical company environment. Wherever you fit on this continuum, remember to have fun and enjoy the exciting times.

Position and Level

Your current and potential value to the organization should determine your position and level. However, there are other considerations besides qualifications, knowledge, skills and abilities. Small pharmaceutical companies are all about acceleration and velocity. How fast can something be done without compromising key quality aspects? How quickly can you get up to speed on a particular set of issues? How rapidly can you add value to the corporate portfolio? How soon can you get answers to key questions that can make or break a development program and allow the most efficient use of limited resources?

The acceleration issue is tied to an understanding of the drug development processes and the garnered ability to anticipate corporate needs. A regulatory professional with these abilities can suggest compliant, accelerating regulatory strategies to shave time off the development or review processes. As discussed above, it is also important to ensure effective communication between you, your peers and senior management to minimize the "silo" effect and potential surprises—especially when you are trying to move quickly.

To advance in position and level, there are a number of things you can strive to do as you gain experience and responsibilities that will help ensure a successful career:

- Find mentors (either within or outside the company) in areas where you do not have expertise.
- Ensure direct interface with your other technical groups (both internally and externally) related to your projects or activities.

Many of the people and groups you meet in your endeavors will become part of your networking base as you mature in the industry. A strong network can increase your value by providing the right contact for an expert answer or referral.

Position Specialties

Specialization within a small pharmaceutical company is generally driven by the size and maturity of the organization. The areas for regulatory specialization are not discrete, and often there is significant overlap. At the most extreme, you may be the only regulatory professional and responsible for all regulatory activities through the use of outside vendors or internal partner groups or alliances. As the company grows, more regulatory resources are generally added.

Typically, the major specialization areas for regulatory professionals are chemistry, manufacturing and controls (CMC), Quality Assurance (QA), nonclinical safety and clinical. A background in science (either chemistry for CMC and QA or biology for nonclinical and clinical) can often support a more rapid understanding of the underlying technical issues and the thinking behind regulatory standards and expectations.

A specialization in CMC focuses on Current Good Manufacturing Practice (CGMP) and related quality control, QA and testing procedures. It requires some chemistry background so you can understand impurity profiles, stability (including forced degradation studies), assay development and validation, and dissolution/bioavailability of both the drug substance and drug product.

The QA function is often considered a separate discipline. It is also important in nonclinical and clinical areas for data accuracy and consistency.

Table 10-1. Summary of Key Knowledge, Skills and Abilities Generally Expected for Increasing Position Seniority

Level/Position	Qualifications	Knowledge	Skills and Abilities
Entry level—Assistant/Associate/Specialist	Bachelor's degree (or certificate)	Scientific process and hypothesis testing	Written and verbal communication Fast assimilation of new information
Advanced level—manager/senior manager/associate director	Bachelor's degree and three to five years' regulatory experience **or** Advanced degree and one to two years' regulatory experience	GxPs and key ICH and FDA guidances Drug development process and associated regulatory requirements	Creating document summaries for different audiences Analysis of relatively complex documents Effective communication in group settings
Advanced level—director/senior director	Bachelor's degree and six to 10 years' regulatory experience **or** Advanced degree and two to six years' regulatory experience	Product label content and underlying strategic considerations Purpose and potential key issues in regulatory agency meetings Experience being the sponsor's primary regulatory contact of record for regulatory agencies	Management of relatively small groups of individuals Understanding your strengths and potential limitations regarding ability and skills and either focusing on your strengths relative to your career path and/or identifying others with the needed skills and abilities you may lack and manage their output Presentation and defense of strategic development plans and timelines Running meetings with in-house senior management, potential licensors or regulatory agency staff Experience with in-house and FDA audits Effective written communication to regulatory agencies Concise summaries of regulatory strategies and information for regulatory agencies or company management Multi-tasking and project management Mentoring

Level/Position	Qualifications	Knowledge	Skills and Abilities
Senior level—Vice president/senior vice president	Bachelor's degree and 10–20+ years' regulatory experience **or** Advanced degree and seven to 12+ years' regulatory experience	Drug development and approval process including special options such as Orphan Drug, fast track, and rolling NDAs "Hot button" issues, options and expectations of FDA divisions most relevant to your current company and therapeutic area(s) Common Technical Document organization and content and the electronic submission process and requirements	Management of larger groups of regulatory professionals including clinical, CMC and auditing Label negotiations with regulatory agencies Presentations at professional meetings and authoring of articles/book chapters Mentoring and coaching skills and maintaining positive and productive interpersonal relationships

If you enjoy methodical approaches that require a good eye for detail, this can be a rewarding area. In many companies, QA includes audit functions to meet auditors' requirements for consistency. This additional dimension may be of interest in a career path.

Nonclinical regulatory areas are often more science background driven, with PhDs in pharmacology and toxicology as well as other specific animal science. You need to understand Good Laboratory Practice (GLP) and be familiar with US Food and Drug Administration (FDA) and International Conference on Harmonisation (ICH) guidelines. Nonclinical requirements include scaling up from preclinical to clinical, understanding how regulatory agencies want data integrated for the Common Technical Document (CTD), designing and interpreting pilot carcinogenicity studies and obtaining FDA input (FDA Special Protocol Assessment (SPA) process), and understanding subtleties of safety pharmacology studies and their translation to human clinical studies and safety profiles.

A regulatory position specializing in clinical can offer significant growth opportunities. These generally focus on understanding the various types of FDA submissions and the underlying regulations and guidelines tied to regulatory agency meetings. Position responsibilities as part of a team or as an individual range chronologically from the pre-IND meeting through IND-related submissions to support clinical studies, as well as communication of safety-related issues, support of other regulatory agency meetings, and specialty aspects such as orphan drug designation requests, fast-track designation requests and SPAs. They end with NDA preparation and submission and post-NDA support. In the current global regulatory environment, this type of position can be a career in itself.

The second type of clinical regulatory position centers on clinical study support. Leading the preparation, conduct and reporting of clinical trials in compliance with ICH Good Clinical Practice (GCP) standards and accomplishing these tasks as quickly as possible involves relatively specific knowledge. Duties can cover writing and reviewing informed consents, creating and maintaining clinical trial master (FDA auditable) files, compiling and reviewing ICH-required appendices for clinical study reports, understanding and providing required documents and translations (with appropriate certifications) for studies conducted outside the US, and reporting requirements and actions needed for Serious Adverse Events (SAEs) and regional clinical study reporting databases.

Moving up the Ladder: How to Advance

Each small pharmaceutical company has its own corporate culture and its senior management team has its own history and personalities. However, in most healthy corporate cultures, certain approaches and attitudes will almost certainly help you advance your career as a regulatory professional. They include understanding your company's assets and goals, adding value to deliverables and keeping a positive team attitude.

One of the enjoyable aspects of a small pharmaceutical company is taking a drug or technology portfolio and figuring out how to add value to it (i.e., save time or money or increase marketability) as quickly as possible. It is important to understand the portfolio and how it is being presented (and viewed) in a competitive development and licensing landscape. You also need to understand how the company is funded (the funding revenue stream and what expectations are attached to it) and how the financial situation is driving company goals and priorities. Finally (also, usually part of the fun), you will be working closely with a small group of senior executives whose immediate futures are tightly aligned with the success of the company. Get to know them as both professionals and people. What drives them? What are their "buttons?" What level of risk are they willing to take (Will they only go with what has worked before or are they willing to consider new approaches)? What is their prior professional experience (including track record of successes and failures) and do they have contract groups or individuals from prior work that they want to retain as part of their new landscape? From a longer-term career perspective, it is not uncommon for development teams who work well together to also move to new companies and positions together.

Once you understand what makes your company valuable and what makes it tick, it is time to understand and exceed expectations. In many small pharmaceutical companies, because things are being invented as they are needed, formalities (including position descriptions, performance evaluations and processes such as formal budgets and budget allocation) are outside the focus of corporate attention. Instead, the primary goal is to add value to the company portfolio as rapidly as possible to ensure a healthy return on investment (ROI). As a regulatory professional, ROI is the mantra that should drive your own performance.

How do you add value to the company and receive credit for it? First, understand the issues and challenges facing development of the company's lead compound(s). If a first-in-class development, careful research is needed and regulatory agency input should be obtained to ensure your approaches are in line with those of the agency. If there are approved compounds in the same class as the one(s) you are developing, leverage this knowledge. However, make sure that you do not blindly copy prior approaches; instead, determine what is unique about your compound or technology or find aspects of that current regulatory and scientific environment that could markedly alter development strategies and options. Timelines can also be shortened by using new approaches and parallel processing of activities and decreased downtime between one series of activities and another. This is especially relevant if the corporate culture encourages significant risk taking, albeit with appropriate contingency plans in place.

In a small pharmaceutical company that has an exciting new portfolio, part of the fun is learning and growing as the organization evolves and matures. You can rapidly increase the breadth and depth of your knowledge. Whether you have made the decision to hire in or contract out certain expertise, you can use internal and external experts to add to your own skills and increase your value to the company. For example, early in my career, my responsibilities encompassed CMC. With only a basic understanding of CMC, I turned to a consulting group that specialized in CMC issues and was able to rapidly learn the specifics of this technical area while using the consulting group to help me develop SOPs and templates for core aspects.

Finally, in an organization that is most likely growing fast, you should remember to train your replacement. As you move up the ladder, you are best served by ensuring the next person in the position knows the ropes and can work with you effectively. This foresight supports your ability to provide positive feedback both up and down the chain of command.

Chapter 11

Working for a Generic Drug Company

By Mary Lou Freathy, JD

The US Food and Drug Administration (FDA) defines a generic drug as "a copy that is the same as a brand-name drug in dosage, safety, strength, how it is taken, quality, performance and intended use."[1]

Generic drug development and approval are somewhat different from the development processes of a brand drug product or "reference listed drug" (RLD). While brand drug discovery requires a large number of professionals from multiple scientific and medical disciplines and the drug itself may require more than 10 years to complete preclinical and clinical phases, a generic copy merely has to show that it is bioequivalent to the RLD. That said, getting a generic product to market can be a very challenging experience because there are many elements that must work together to bring the product to market. A regulatory professional must understand the basic requirements for generic drugs and the specific manufacturing or clinical requirements for certain types of products as well as patent and exclusivity details that may provide information about how the drug should be formulated or packaged and what type of submission must be filed.

Generic drugs are less expensive than brand-name drugs simply because generic manufacturers do not have the same high expenses as brand-name drug companies. There is a considerable investment in developing a new drug. A new drug must be safe and effective. This means that studies must be performed to show safety and efficacy. The studies, or clinical trials, are very costly and very time intensive. A generic company does not have the same costs associated with drug discovery because that work has already been done. On the other hand, a generic product also must be safe and effective. Pursuant to US law, a generic equivalent must be formulated using the same amount of active ingredient, in the same dosage form and using the same route of administration as the brand-name drug. The final product must be found by FDA to have the same therapeutic safety, efficacy and performance characteristics as its brand-name counterpart.

One of the biggest challenges in the generic business is getting the Abbreviated New Drug Application (ANDA) filed as quickly as possible, before other generic competitors. In some cases FDA will grant an exclusivity period to the generic version that is the first of its kind filed for approval. When a generic firm successfully proves that the RLD patent is no longer valid or is not infringed by its generic formula, FDA may reward the firm with 180 days of exclusive marketing rights.

How a Generic Drug Is Born

Formulation scientists begin by reverse engineering the RLD to create the generic copy. This means that the scientist must determine what the RLD is composed of and at what levels, and characterize the active ingredient.

The generic formulation must be manufactured using the same active ingredient as the RLD and must match the RLD within tight acceptance criteria. At the same time, the generic formulation must circumvent any patent restrictions on the brand-name drug formula.

The generic formulation must be bioequivalent to the brand-name drug formula; this equivalence allows FDA to presume it will be safe and effective, and presents no significant difference from the brand-name product. The generic manufacturer must demonstrate by either *in vitro* (laboratory testing) or *in vivo* (human testing), or both, that the drug becomes "available" at the site of action at the same rate as the brand-name drug. If bioavailability can be shown without human studies, the generic firm can request a bio-waiver. These decisions are generally made jointly by the company's clinical specialists and formulation and analytical chemists.

Analytical methods must be developed and validated by analytical chemists to test the generic drug product.

Once a formulation is demonstrated to match the RLD through experimental batches, an "exhibit" batch (also referred to as a bio-batch or ANDA batch) is manufactured. This is the batch that will be tested for bioequivalence and for stability to collect data required for filing an ANDA.

Using bioequivalence as the basis for approving generic copies of drug products was established by the *Drug Price Competition and Patent Term Restoration Act* of 1984, also known as the *Hatch-Waxman Act*. Brand-name drugs are subject to the same bioequivalence tests as generics when their manufacturers reformulate them.[3]

Where Does the Regulatory Professional Fit in?

In the generic world, time is money because the main goal of a generic manufacturer is to have the first generic product on the market.

Regulatory professionals participate in every step of the process. They offer guidance on regulatory requirements and filing decision making. Regulatory strategy is a very important part of the selection and development process for a proposed generic. A good regulatory professional will be able to help identify barriers to filing an ANDA that will be accepted for review by FDA. It is critical to know whether an ANDA is acceptable because many other things are attached to or calculated from the FDA acceptance date. For example, FDA's chemistry, manufacturing and controls (CMC), microbiology, labeling and bioequivalence review processes, and the notification to a patent holder that an ANDA has been filed are all based upon the FDA acceptance date. Only the first generic product approved is eligible for the 180-day exclusivity period, so it is important to file an acceptable ANDA as early as possible.

When FDA's Office of Generic Drugs receives an ANDA, the assigned project manager goes through a checklist (available on the generic drugs page of the FDA website, www.fda.gov) to ensure that all elements required for the filing are included. Once FDA determines that the ANDA is acceptable, it will send the generic firm, or sponsor, an "Acceptance for Filing" letter indicating that the ANDA has been passed on to the review divisions. If the ANDA is missing required or critical information, the sponsor will receive a not-so-nice communication called a "Refuse-To-Receive" (RTR) letter stating that the ANDA is not acceptable. In this case, the sponsor must correct the deficiencies and re-file the response. In the case of an RTR, the clock starts over.

There are many roles in the regulatory arena of generic drugs. The following are some specific organizational considerations and an exploration of the roles of the regulatory professional in a generic products organization:

Organizational Considerations

Some regulatory departments divide themselves into a preapproval group and a postapproval group. The preapproval group is primarily responsible for submitting ANDA filings, along with CMC review and labeling. The postapproval group handles activities associated with products that have already been approved and commercialized, such as Annual Reports, adverse event reporting, labeling and advertising and supplements to approved products.

Companies may also have a separate regulatory group for handling site transfer activities. When a company performs a manufacturing site transfer of a product from one company to another, FDA must approve the transfer before the product made at the new site can be marketed.

A more traditional way to organize a regulatory group is by product or product line. A group of generalists handles everything, including the preapproval review and filing and postapproval commercial activities. This approach works well when there are only a few products and growth is expected to be minimal. But when a generic company is trying to file as many applications as possible (the most common business model) it can be more efficient to organize a group that handles original filings only. The benefits are better focus and efficiency: the filings get top priority without having to compete with postapproval activities.

Many regulatory departments also have a technical role associated with electronic submissions.

No matter how a generic drug company's regulatory department is organized, it normally includes some or all of these positions: regulatory specialist, associate, analyst, CMC specialist and project manager. There are various levels of each of the positions (such as "Senior Associate," "Project Manager 2" or "Associate Director"), so there is plenty of opportunity for growth and advancement. These positions usually report to a manager or director and are described in detail in the next section.

Position Specialties

As with a brand-name drug company, it is essential that the generic regulatory professional have a strong scientific or technical background. Although it is not a requirement that the regulatory professional have a master's degree or PhD, it is becoming more commonplace for generic companies to prefer those who have advanced degrees. Minimally, companies want to hire individuals with bachelor's degrees and Regulatory Affairs Certification (RAC) in drugs. These qualifications help ensure that the regulatory professional has the ability to understand scientific and technical details, and the ability to analyze information presented and evaluate its impact. In this era of economic unrest, there are and will be an abundance of excellent candidates to choose from in selecting the right person for the position, so it is critical that the regulatory professional stay in touch with the regulatory development process through training and professional meetings, i.e. GPhA.[4]

Another very important qualification, and one of the most important in the generic field, is the ability to manage projects. Regulatory professionals must constantly juggle multiple projects and priorities, and must be organized and flexible enough to change gears with a moment's notice.

Some of the specializations within the generic regulatory department are: labeling and advertising, CMC, ANDA filings, postapproval filings, clinical, ADE reporting, and compliance (field alerts and recalls).

Because so many generic companies work with outside partners, there may be opportunities to work with regulatory professionals at other companies, both domestic and international, and some travel may be involved.

Table 11-1 lists basic qualifications for some standard regulatory positions at a generic drug company. The grid is arranged from the most-junior to the most-senior position. Since there are no industry standards for positions, both the titles and the requirements will vary by company.

Qualifications, Knowledge, Skills and Abilities

It is essential that the generic regulatory professional possess a strong scientific or technical background, the ability to understand scientific and technical details, and the ability to analyze this type of information. A critical qualification in the generic drug field is the ability to effectively manage project activities and associated teams. Additional requirements are:

- working knowledge of FDA and international regulations
- proficiency in preparing FDA regulatory submissions and documents for product marketing approval
- thorough understanding of and experience with product development and manufacturing
- strong organizational, project management, interpersonal and written and oral communication skills

Moving up the Ladder: How to Advance

One of the best ways to move up the ladder in a generic drug company is to learn as many functions as possible and to understand the whole picture of generic drug product development, not just a specific discipline.

Doing this will show that you are ambitious and willing to work hard and do what it takes to get the job done. Take advantage of opportunities that come your way, whether or not they are part of your job description or area of comfort. Take advantage of learning opportunities, even if they mean giving up a lunch hour or staying late at the office. Ask to attend relevant industry seminars and meetings. Always be proactive and do not wait for your supervisor to organize your training. In the ever-changing regulatory environment, it is

Table 11-1. Basic Qualifications for Regulatory Positions at Generic Drug Companies

Title	Education	Experience	Supervision	Other
Specialist	Bachelor's degree, preferably in a scientific discipline	Two to four years of regulatory experience	Entry level	Technical writing skills
Associate	Bachelor's degree, preferably in a scientific discipline	Five to eight years of regulatory experience. Specific experience in filing ANDAs. Familiarity with FDA regulations	Independent	RAC (drugs) preferred. Excellent writing skills
Regulatory project manager	Bachelor's degree, preferably in a scientific discipline	Five to eight years of related RA experience or two to four years with a master's degree	Minimal; able to supervise	RAC (drugs) preferred. Excellent project management skills
CMC specialist	Bachelor's degree in a scientific discipline. PhD preferred	Seven to 11 years' experience in the pharmaceutical industry with at least three years in a regulatory function	Independent	Experience or prior training in quality or manufacturing is helpful
Director	Master's or PhD preferred	Five to 10 years of generic drug RA experience	Directly supervises	RAC (drugs) preferred. Excellent leadership skills

critically important for the regulatory professional to continually develop new skills. You can learn about the requirements and precedents related to generic drugs by doing Internet research; a great deal of information is available on the FDA website (www.fda.gov).

Another important skill to accelerate your move up the ladder in a generic company is to show that you can step into your supervisor's shoes if needed. Volunteer. Show your enthusiasm. The industry wants upbeat, ambitious and enthusiastic leaders. Do not be frustrated by having to pay your dues by starting at the bottom. In the long run, you will not regret learning on the job or the substantial time you put in along the way. Last but not least, persevere!

You will get a promotion, even if you have to be patient for a little while due to corporate circumstances.

Summary

Many of the qualifications for regulatory professionals in branded and generic drug companies are similar. Generic company regulatory professionals often have more CMC experience than others, but it is not mandatory. Generic regulatory professionals also need to have a good understanding of regulations and the creative ability to work through patents and exclusivity to benefit their company.

Generic companies are a good career choice for many regulatory professionals because they are expected to capture a larger share of the market in the future.

References

1. US Food and Drug Administration. Generic Drugs: Questions and Answers. www.fda.gov/Drugs/ResourcesForYou/Consumers/QuestionsAnswers/ucm100100.htm. Accessed 18 August 2010.
2. 21 CFR §314.94.
3. US Department of Health and Human Services Public Health Service, Food and Drug Administration.
4. The Generic Pharmaceutical Association. (GPhA) represents the manufacturers and distributors of finished generic pharmaceutical products, manufacturers and distributors of bulk active pharmaceutical chemicals, and suppliers of other goods and services to the generic pharmaceutical industry. www.gphaonline.org.

CHAPTER 12

Specializing in Regulatory Chemistry, Manufacturing and Controls

By Joseph Greer, RAC

The chemistry, manufacturing and controls (CMC) section makes up about one-third of a New Drug Application (NDA) and two-thirds of an Abbreviated New Drug Application (ANDA). An NDA requires a full description of the composition, manufacture and specifications under 21 CFR 314.50(d)(1), and for an ANDA, the same information is required as described under 21 CFR 314.94. Both must include information on the drug substance, drug product composition and formulation, excipients, stability, packaging components and comparative studies, where applicable.

Responsibilities of the Specialist

CMC specialists are responsible for the submission of the CMC portion of NDAs and ANDAs for approval by the US Food and Drug Administration (FDA). The submission process encompasses compilation, preparation and technical review and requires scientific knowledge of both the product's chemistry and the production process (manufacturing and controls).

The CMC specialist is responsible for responding to FDA deficiency letters, writing scientific justifications based upon applicable regulatory guidelines, and working with manufacturing and testing sites to develop and improve their GMP infrastructure as it relates to regulatory activities and systems to ensure compliance and successful FDA inspections. The CMC specialist also maintains approved applications through annual reporting and supplements.

In addition to NDAs and ANDAs, there are several other types of submissions, both preapproval and postapproval, which require CMC review by the CMC specialist:

Preapproval
- Drug Master File (DMF)
- Investigational New Drug Application (IND)
- Biologics License Application (BLA)
- Premarket Approval Application (PMA)
- 510(k) Premarket Notification

Postapproval
- Postmarket supplements
- Annual Reports

These FDA filings cover a multitude of pharmaceutical products including active pharmaceutical ingredients, tablets, capsules, solutions, suspensions, parenterals, sterile suspensions, lyophilized products, nasal sprays, transdermals and ophthalmics. They also cover biopharmaceutical and biologic products.

Typical responsibilities of the CMC specialist include but are not limited to:

Preapproval:
- planning, writing and coordinating the preparation of the CMC portion of regulatory dossier submissions (including INDs, IND amendments, BLAs, NDAs, ANDAs) in accordance with the regulations and relevant guidelines (national and international) in a cross-functional team setting according to strict timelines and with attention to optimal quality
- providing CMC regulatory expertise to the manufacturing group and all cross-functional project teams with regard to CMC regulations pertaining to development of pharmaceutical drug products for the US and international registration
- advising on additional CMC requirements for transitioning from Phase 2 to Phase 3 compounds and ultimate commercialization
- producing high quality regulatory submissions using electronic publishing systems
- preparing labeling with full prescribing information

Postapproval:
- providing CMC regulatory strategy to ensure a speedy approval pathway for manufacturing changes, such as new suppliers of

ingredients or manufacturing site changes to marketed products
- Preparing and/or reviewing and approving routine regulatory submissions, including Annual Reports, periodic safety reports and expedited safety reports, as necessary

The specialist is also responsible for developing and maintaining a Quality Assurance/compliance structure for regulatory submissions in accordance with the firm's overall quality/compliance structure.

The specialist's duties regarding quality and compliance can encompass the following:
- conducting due diligence audits (The CMC specialist represents regulatory in due diligence activities as required, writing reports and providing recommendations.)
- conducting Current Good Manufacturing Practice (CGMP), quality system and preapproval audits of manufacturers and vendors to ensure a successful FDA inspection for pending applications
- providing guidance related to FDA regulations, policies and procedures
- providing guidance on import procedures
- participating in recalls

Based upon audit findings, the specialist may work with manufacturing and testing sites to develop and improve their GMP infrastructure as it relates to regulatory activities to ensure compliance with GMPs and to ensure successful preapproval inspections.

CMC Strategy

An effective strategy to achieve CMC compliance is vital to ensure a smooth FDA review and approval of an application. CMC deficiencies result in delays in approval. CMC regulatory compliance deficiencies of marketed products have also resulted in FDA Warning Letters and product recalls. At each stage of the process, from drug discovery to Phase 1 and through market approval, the CMC specialist must ask, "What is required from a CMC compliance perspective in order be successful?"

In developing the CMC strategy, it is important to be aware of the company's goals and objectives, the stage of development for each product and the capabilities of the company or the manufacturer who will be used.

Experience is a key factor in a successful strategy. Seasoned CMC specialists who have been exposed to a variety of situations involving regulatory strategy, interaction with FDA, and preparation of submissions can identify issues and provide appropriate solutions. Foreseeing potential consequences of strategies laid out for submissions comes from experience with FDA. Understanding the agency's expectations is not always easy, as these expectations may not be spelled out clearly in guidances and other documents. When compliance issues arise with FDA, the specialist can use knowledge of FDA regulations and experience with agency thinking to provide advice and assistance to resolve the agency's concern.

From a tactical standpoint, the specialist should establish a clearly defined process for the preparation, assembly and review of CMC documentation to be submitted in an application, and be able to carry out the procedures required for investigational, pre- and postapproval applications. Identifying the appropriate documentation in the beginning will prevent potential issues later. CMC specialists should have a checklist describing the deliverables for the submission along with timeframes for completion. Specific target dates should include turnaround times for review, correction, and compilation of documents for the final submission.

Overview of the CMC Section Preparation Process

The CMC specialist should be able to prepare CMC sections for all types of applications for agencies both in the US and elsewhere and DMFs covering both bulk drug and final drug products.

For products intended for marketing in multiple countries, it is important that the requirements of these regions be considered as early as possible, as they will have an impact on development and specifications. For example, some countries require Site Master Files. This registration documentation is submitted directly to the applicable regulatory agency.

Overview of the CMC Review Process

CMC reviews are performed by the CMC specialist to achieve a successful filing at the agency. The CMC review is based upon an understanding of the science and technology related to the product and manufacturing process being submitted to the agency for approval.

Each type of submission requires a comprehensive scientific assessment performed by a highly trained specialist to determine whether the submission is complete and accurate for its intended purpose. To carry out the review function effectively, the CMC specialist should have a scientific and technical background. This is necessary in order to perform a scientific evaluation of the information comprising the CMC portion of the submission, and understand the product and its performance, the manufacturing process involved and Quality Assurance systems designed to ensure a high quality product. The CMC specialist must be able to spot scientific errors and work with experts to ensure the data provided are accurate.

Besides a scientific background, the specialist must have an extensive regulatory background. The CMC compilation and review should encompass FDA's current regulatory requirements and incorporate the agency's risk-based approach to submissions to ensure an acceptable filing and quick approval.

The specialist has many tools at his or her disposal of which he or she must have knowledge and experience:
- regulations
- FDA guidance
- FDA Manuals of Policies and Procedures (MaPPs)

It is important that the specialist understand the difference between each, and recognize that these tools are fundamental to addressing CMC issues and getting a submission through FDA's review process as quickly and efficiently as possible. The goal is to minimize any requests from FDA for additional data and information. Knowledge of precedents set by FDA to understand decisions made by the agency, and how issues have been handled historically, are also important when performing the CMC review.

CMC specialists must have the technical expertise, regulatory expertise and other skills required to evaluate whether:
- the CMC review document is accurate and clear, with scientific bases for conclusions made in the submission
- FDA policies and regulations have been followed

The CMC review process performed by a specialist should yield a written list of issues that would benefit from further assessment by company experts. Each issue noted should identify the group that is able to provide further input on the matter.

Due to the technical complexity of CMC reviews, CMC specialists need to be exposed to emerging technologies and science so they are familiar with the issues and prepared to discuss issues found during review.

Acquiring Skills to Become a Specialist

First and foremost, CMC specialists should demonstrate an extensive knowledge of regulations and guidances for relevant FDA divisions and/or other geographic regions for all stages of the development process for the type of drug manufactured by their company, and be able to communicate these requirements and practices to the appropriate corporate groups. To gain the required knowledge, a junior specialist should work with someone with extensive experience to answer deficiency letters and negotiate with various FDA reviewing divisions. It takes several years for a CMC specialist to acquire the experience to develop successful regulatory strategies for achieving approval for the various types of dosage forms.

A new specialist can be assigned to postapproval submissions while learning the requirements for a submission. This can include compilation, review and submission of supplements (changes being effected (CBE), changes being effected in 30 days (CBE-30), labeling), Annual Reports, drug listings and all other required regulatory postapproval submissions to FDA. The specialist can also assist with the review, compilation and submission of prior approval supplements. The specialist will learn to prepare all submissions in accordance with current FDA requirements and learn to interact with quality control, Quality Assurance, manufacturing and other pertinent functional areas throughout the process to ensure all documents are reviewed, all problems are identified and addressed, and the submissions are assembled in accordance with established timelines. Specialists can also learn how to interface with contract manufacturers to assess requirements for third-party supplements. Maintenance of regulatory files will help in acquiring the appropriate regulatory knowledge required for future submissions.

Joining various regulatory professional organizations, such as the Regulatory Affairs Professional Society (RAPS), and attending regulatory conferences help the new specialist understand current FDA thinking.

Fitting into the Company and Interacting with other Departments

The ultimate responsibility for the contents of a submission's CMC section lies with the subject matter experts in research and development (R&D), manufacturing, etc. However, input from the specialist ensures that appropriate data are generated and gathered for a successful submission. That is why, once a product has been identified and a project initiated, the CMC specialist must become part of the product development team. Participation will allow the specialist to identify the data that must be obtained for inclusion in the CMC section and to perform an evaluation to determine their impact on the submission. It also enables any modifications to the CMC regulatory strategy early in the process.

In dealing with cross-functional teams, the specialist must be flexible and maintain an understanding of all activities and their durations and work with the project teams when delays can impact the overall project timeline. One of the most critical aspects to a successful working relationship between the specialist and the expert groups is open communication. It is vital that all issues be identified and shared openly.

The CMC specialist also serves as the company resource for CMC requirements and industry trends and evaluates the regulatory impact of GMP compliance and CMC validation issues. The specialist should provide technical writing assistance to authors of submission documents as needed.

Considerations for Specializing in This Area

CMC specialists must have an adequate scientific understanding of products and processes, in addition to a regulatory background. Following are desirable qualifications:

- a bachelor's degree in chemistry, biochemistry or related field (master's, doctorate or PharmD a plus)
- several years experience in regulatory
- solid working knowledge of drug development process and FDA regulatory requirements and guidelines
- ability to develop, write, compile and review regulatory submissions, yearly updates, risk management and evaluation plans and other supplements
- ability to develop domestic and international regulatory strategic plans and recommend optimal national and international requirements for each
- ability to prepare electronic Common Technical Document (eCTD) submissions in collaboration with eCTD vendors and convert current submissions to CTD or eCTD
- experience dealing with other agencies—EU, Canada and other countries
- demonstrated experience leading submission teams for NDA, ANDA, BLA, IND, DMF, etc.
- experience interacting with regulatory authorities on a regular basis, including preparing packages for milestone meetings such as End-of-Phase 2 and teleconferences, and planning, coordinating and conducting these meetings
- strong project management, problem-solving, negotiating, interpersonal and communication skills (both written and oral)

CHAPTER 13

A Career in Promotional Regulatory

By Kimberly Carneal

To understand what a career in promotional regulatory might entail, you must first understand the industry environment for this particular specialty area. Regardless of corporate structure or product portfolio, pharmaceutical companies are heavily scrutinized in many areas pertaining to how they market and sell to healthcare professionals and consumers.

Companies must comply with all of the laws, rules and regulations that govern advertising, promotion and sale of prescription products. To do so, these companies must ensure the highest integrity and accuracy of all data and claims in communications disseminated to healthcare professionals, patients, caregivers, payers and regulators.

The marketing and sale of prescription products are highly regulated by the US Food and Drug Administration (FDA). FDA controls virtually every aspect of prescription products and can impose serious and costly sanctions against a company for regulatory violations. These sanctions range from Notice of Violation and Warning Letters to product seizures and fines and criminal prosecution.

In general, FDA considers all mentions, descriptions or promotions of a product to be regulated as labeling, promotion or advertising, regardless of whether oral or in writing and regardless of media type, including printed materials, events, etc.

FDA is not the only regulator or critic of the pharmaceutical industry. The Office of Inspector General (OIG), the Department of Justice (DOJ), the media, company stockholders, healthcare professionals and consumers are all concerned with how a company is conducting its marketing and sales activities.

As a promotional regulatory professional, you are in a position to help ensure that your company's marketing and sales activities stay within the bounds of legal and ethical behavior. Accomplishing this task may not always be as simple as it sounds. In addition to having a good understanding of the regulations, you will need to stay abreast of the legal environment and enforcement activities while balancing all of this against your company's goals and objectives.

One of your primary responsibilities will be to review all of the advertising and promotional materials for your company. These materials may be branded with specific product information and claims or they may be disease-related, i.e., discussing a particular disease without mentioning the product name. The focus of your review will be to ensure that all promotional messages are in compliance with FDA regulations as well as other applicable federal, state and local laws and regulations.

The Review Process

Each company will have or should establish review processes specific to its corporate needs and structure. Most companies have some type of cross-functional review team, which may be called a promotional review board (PRB) or a medical, legal and regulatory team (MLR). The review board or team generally includes representatives from marketing, medical or clinical affairs, legal and regulatory. Other *ad hoc* members may be invited, depending upon the company's specific review requirements and resources. For example, a reimbursement specialist may be asked to help review marketing material related to Medicare/Medicaid or other types of insurance coverage.

Typically, either the marketing representative or the promotional regulatory professional leads the meeting. An individual will be assigned as the coordinator for activities associated with the review and approval of marketing materials. The coordinator's responsibilities will include assigning product codes to pieces, tracking the status of materials under review, scheduling review meetings, distributing materials for review including any reference materials needed to verify claims being made, and collecting comments and signatures for approval. Once the review and approval process is complete, this person is also responsible for obtaining from marketing, the final package of approved materials for the regulatory department to send to FDA's Division of Drug, Marketing, Advertising and Communications (DDMAC).

The originator of the materials (usually someone from marketing, sales or corporate communications) is responsible for ensuring they are routed through the PRB/MLR for review and approval. In cases where marketing also leads the review meetings, it might seem like an odd power advantage to have control over discussion of their own materials. The potential conflict can be avoided by a policy requiring sign-off by all review team members.

Medical or clinical affairs team members are responsible for reviewing the materials to ensure they are medically accurate and either truly representative of the clinical trials and patient populations studied (for submissions) or appropriate for use in investigator and/or patient recruitment.

Legal is responsible for ensuring that the materials are in compliance with state and federal laws and regulations and corporate policies. For example, legal would be concerned with any material that has a negative impact on Security and Exchange Commission (SEC) filings or that will potentially implicate the *Fair Trade Act* or *Lanham Act* as well as any other non-FDA specific law or regulation that the company must be in compliance with. This activity includes ensuring contractual requirements are followed, identifying and evaluating potential risks involving patient and/or product liability issues associated with use of the materials and assessing patent and trademark issues.

The regulatory representative on this cross-functional team is responsible for ensuring that the materials are consistent with FDA-approved labeling (i.e., on-label), are not false or misleading and are fairly balanced. This involves verifying that all data and claims used are appropriate, accurate and consistent with the approved labeling, appropriate regulations, guidelines and the company's policies. Another responsibility is determining whether approved materials are required to be submitted to DDMAC. Any materials mentioning a prescription drug product by name and created for the purpose of promoting it must be submitted to DDMAC at the time of dissemination. Disease-related materials are not required to be submitted. If required, you will be responsible for preparing and sending the submission. Once the submission has been sent, you will be responsible for notifying marketing that the approved materials may be disseminated.

One of the more popular methods for reviewing marketing materials is a meeting of the PRB/MLR. Materials are sent to team members a few days or a week in advance of the meeting. They are responsible for reviewing the materials and coming to the meeting prepared to discuss their comments. You and the team should provide guidance to the marketing representatives on any required or suggested changes to reduce the risk of disseminating violative materials. There may be times when the team cannot reach agreement. Companies should establish a procedure for handling conflict resolution. This process often involves senior or executive management hearing opposing views and making a decision.

Once the team has discussed the individual comments and agreed on the final text, the coordinator will either change the document electronically during the meeting or capture the changes manually and change the final document later.

Other companies may route materials to each team member for review sequentially or in parallel. Comments are then collected and collated as necessary and comments addressed as appropriate.

Types of Materials to be Reviewed

One of the most frequent questions you will be asked is, "Does this need to be reviewed by the promotional review board?" The quick regulatory answer is, "It depends," but in the long run it is better to begin answering the question by asking a series of other questions.

The real answer to the question depends upon the content of the piece and its intended audience. You will need to find out whether the piece references the marketed product directly or through implication, i.e., if the piece is branded. Next, you should ask how the piece will be used. For example, an item such as a detail aid (i.e., a sales brochure) for use with healthcare professionals is definitely a piece that should be reviewed by the PRB. A slide presentation for use at an investigator's meeting may not require this type of review but may be subject to another review, depending upon your company's policies and procedures.

While it would be hard to list each piece that requires review, there are specific categories of materials that should be reviewed by the promotional review board:

- materials developed for written or oral promotional use via any medium or form (e.g., direct-to-consumer mailings, TV or journal ads, blog postings, email communications and giveaways, and signage and booths at medical events
- materials that will be distributed by the sales force
- corporate communication materials containing product information (e.g., corporate website, press releases, press kits)

FDA considers any communications and/or materials that specifically mention or imply the use of a prescription product to be regulated as labeling, promotion or advertising. To avoid a mention or implication, the PRB should evaluate disease-related advertising materials, such as corporate communications containing disease-related information and reprints of journal articles intended for use by the sales force. The purpose is to ensure that disease-related communications do not cross over into promotional materials. For example, a disease campaign should not use the same colors and graphic design as the branded promotional campaign.

Areas of Regulatory Concern for Sales and Marketing

In today's changing regulatory environment, and when the rules cannot be explained in "black and white" terms, it is easy to slip into areas that are open to interpretation. A tremendous amount of scrutiny is being focused on the pharmaceutical industry by the federal government and the media to ensure that relationships with healthcare professionals and consumers are appropriate and that products are promoted in a way that is consistent with the approved labeling (i.e., no off-label promotion). The primary concern is that pharmaceutical companies are inappropriately influencing healthcare professionals by offering gifts or other monetary incentives (i.e., remuneration) in exchange for prescribing or purchasing drugs. Because of the inappropriate behavior of some companies and individuals as well as bad publicity, consumers are more aware of internal marketing strategies and have built up quite a bit of skepticism and mistrust regarding pharmaceutical companies.

The best advice is to ensure that you are aware of all of the sales and marketing activities undertaken by your company and how each relates to the others. Assessing the risk for each activity individually and in combination will help ensure that the company is behaving responsibly and in compliance with FDA regulations and federal, state and local statutes, as well as its own corporate policies. Although a single problematic situation can trigger an investigation, it is usually a combination of activities plus intent that can lead to subpoenas, indictments, settlements and convictions.

A promotional regulatory professional is responsible for assessing the risks of sales and marketing activities and providing advice on the best course of action. Part of your assessment will include the level of risk (high, medium or low) that a particular event or activity may present. In determining the level of risk, you should estimate its likelihood of occurring and the consequences. Your company's management must determine (and you will need to understand) its tolerance for risk and associated consequences (i.e., receipt of a Notice of Violation Letter or Warning Letter requiring cessation of certain activities or performance of corrective action or, in the worst case, a criminal investigation or indictment or product seizure).

Open and honest communication with the marketing and sales departments is critical to success as a promotional regulatory professional. In the long run, it is critical to their success as well. Understanding marketing and sales objectives and the plan of action will enable you to identify potential risk areas before they become real problems. In your role, you will be able to help them meet their goals and objectives while operating within the appropriate boundaries of regulations and company policies and procedures.

It is also wise to pay special attention to areas where current regulatory or political interest is focused, such as direct-to-consumer (DTC) campaigns, promotional speaker programs and medical/scientific conventions and exhibits.

New Challenges in DTC Advertising

Consumers seek information about particular medical problems to help them better understand treatment options and communicate more effectively with doctors and other healthcare professionals. The Internet has drastically changed the traditional doctor-patient relationship. Instead of deferring to their physicians, consumers are now researching medical information and demanding to be partners in their own healthcare. Consumers who read something on the Internet about a particular product often ask their doctors for additional information, clarification and possibly a prescription. DTC advertising has been used extensively by the industry to reach large numbers of consumers (and potential patients) to educate them about available prescription products and generate demand.

Until recently, DTC advertising consisted largely of direct mailings to consumers, television and radio advertisements and websites. A new era in DTC advertising dawned with the rise of social media such as Facebook, My Space, Twitter and You Tube. Companies find themselves in uncharted waters without clear guidance or precedents for utilizing social media in compliance with promotional regulations, most of which were written long before the widespread use of the Internet.

FDA has recognized that advertising in different media does require a company to use different approaches to meet the promotional regulations. Therefore, the agency has issued guidance on different techniques, such as a "brief summary" of risk information for print ads and a "major statement" of risk information along with "adequate provision" for obtaining full product labeling in broadcast advertisements. While FDA has yet to issue formal rules for marketing drugs on the Internet, it continues to insist that its concerns with specific materials would relate to the message and not the medium. According to a recent article in *The Washington Post*, FDA is closely monitoring the development of these new ways of communicating with consumers.

In November 2009, FDA held a two-day public hearing to learn how the industry was using the Internet and social media to promote products.

The pharmaceutical industry has been slow to take full advantage of the opportunities social networking can provide because of the uncertainty of how to address the potential regulatory and legal issues. Social media is a community-based network or culture where members often have candid conversations about the topic at hand. Social media has the potential to offer benefits to any marketing program. For example, social media provides a mechanism for posting late-breaking news as well as to have conversations directly with consumers or to monitor conversations between consumers. The success of a social media campaign depends upon the ability to have a user-friendly site with the resources available to quickly respond to posts by users.

Social media can be branded or unbranded. For example, a YouTube video or Twitter feed would more than likely be considered promotional by FDA if it were company-sponsored and contained the product name, indication and claims. A discussion board on a disease-related website would probably not be considered promotional even if product names are mentioned, as long as the company is not participating in the discussion.

One of the main dilemmas your company will face is how to ensure compliance with promotional regulations in a medium where you will not have full control over the content of conversations (like a discussion board). Even though the site may be designed to be disease-related, it is highly possible that users of the site will have product-related discussions. It is also possible that these discussions may cover uses for the product outside of your approved labeling (i.e., off-label).

One of the key factors in determining whether a piece is promotional or not (aside from the product name, indication and claims being made), is deciding how involved the company will be in the creation and control of content. It is important to note that even if a company does not create content but is involved in the editing process, the piece is likely to be considered promotional because the company has a level of control over the content. Executives and staff should be trained on potential risk areas and the need to monitor and report any adverse events. A strategy on how to respond to negative or inaccurate online commentary should be created.

The role of the promotional regulatory professional is challenging and requires constant diligence in monitoring activities of your company, other companies, FDA and other regulatory bodies. Because FDA is concerned with the message and not the mode of the communication, you must continually find a way to balance the company's business objectives with rules and regulations to stay out of trouble.

As an example, suppose your marketing team would like to start a Facebook page to raise awareness about National [*insert disease*] Awareness Month. The focus of the campaign will be to educate readers on the disease and its impact on patients. This sounds like a wonderful community outreach program for your company. The PRB will need to review the Facebook page and understand how information will be posted and monitored.

Specifically, you must review the content of the webpage to understand the layout and make sure that all text and associated graphics remain nonpromotional. Since Facebook pages offer a mechanism for "fans" to discuss postings, you will need to understand how the page will be monitored. Any reference to adverse events must be investigated and reported as required.

Companies can mitigate the risks associated with disease-awareness fan pages and discussion boards by developing corporate policies that dictate the level of involvement the company will exert in the creation, review and monitoring of content. A "terms of use" policy should be created and shared with visitors of the site to explain how their postings will be monitored, possibly edited and/or deleted. Staff members and/or consultants who are tasked with monitoring the site should be educated on what might be considered off-label text and how to identify adverse event postings. There should be a policy on handling off-label references or adverse event postings. The company may find that it has to turn the disease-related page into a branded page in order to address off-label postings and provide adequate, fair coverage of the safety and risk information.

For a branded social media piece (i.e., the copy, including text, ads, etc. that will be placed on a social media site), you would face similar regulatory issues: ensuring that the piece is and remains on-label, fairly balanced, and not false or misleading. The amount of preparation and review involved in keeping the branded site in compliance with promotional regulations should be discussed. Careful consideration should be given to your available resources before venturing into branded social media.

Building a Successful Review Team

In this industry, you may often hear marketing and sales staff refer disparagingly to their coworkers in regulatory, legal and/or compliance as "Sales Prevention." The key to building a successful review team is effective, consistent, open and honest communication with marketing and sales staff to emphasize that you are not preventing sales; you are protecting the company and its interests. By understanding the regulatory landscape, the current legal enforcement environment and the company's goals and objectives, you bring value to the review team.

Working in an area without "black and white" rules can be stressful at times. You may be presented with extremely creative marketing campaigns that require in-depth regulatory analysis to determine potential risks and teamwork to mitigate the risks. However, working closely with marketing and sales—in essence, becoming part of those groups—helps you achieve visibility, use creativity in helping to structure compliant messages, and learn about the activities of sales and marketing. Plus, you have the satisfaction of working toward a worthy goal——to sell the company's products and to improve the lives of the patients who take them.

References
1. According to 21 CFR 314.81(b)(3)(i), all advertisements and promotional labeling for a particular drug product must be submitted at the time of initial publication or dissemination. Each submission is required to be accompanied by a completed transmittal Form FDA-2253. US Food and Drug Administration. DDMAC Form FDA-2253 submissions. www.fda.gov/AboutFDA/CentersOffices/CDER/ucm090181.htm. Accessed 19 August 2010.
2. Lunzer Kritz F. "Drug Firms Jockey for Space Online," *The Washington* Post, 16 June 2009. www.washingtonpost.com/wp-dyn/content/article/2009/06/12/AR2009061203230.html. Accessed 19 August 2010.

CHAPTER 14

Alternative Career Pathways in Regulatory

By Theresa M. Straut, CIP, RAC

The clinical research enterprise holds many career opportunities, and the area of entry into the field may not necessarily be the same you would pursue as a lifelong profession. While scientific and clinical training may accelerate advancement, there are many sectors of the research enterprise where you may enjoy a full and rewarding work experience in a growth-oriented environment. One such sector is the regulatory field.

In the private sector, a regulatory career traditionally begins with an entry-level position at a pharmaceutical, biotechnology or device company. This entry level job may be in "regulatory" or "clinical (administrative)" and involve support for preclinical (laboratory/animal) research or clinical research (involving human subjects).

An individual may actually be working in regulatory before even being aware that there is such an entity as a regulatory professional. In "Regulatory Affairs Professional Development," a white paper released by the Regulatory Affairs Professional Society (RAPS) in 2007, regulatory professionals are defined by the tasks they are involved in rather than by particular education, training or experience. According to the white paper, regulatory professionals:

"play critical roles throughout the product lifecycle…they provide strategic, tactical and operational direction and support for working with the regulations to expedite the development and delivery of safe and effective healthcare products…".

This broad definition encompasses more than just the usual and customary activities relating to submission of data to regulatory agencies as part of the approval cycle. Once in the field, you can advance within the organization or work in an organization where the scope of duties and responsibilities can be as wide-ranging as the imagination can envision.

A brief review of my own career path, including government contracting, pharmaceutical/biologic/device development and protection of human subjects participating in biomedical or social/behavioral science research, illustrates the breadth of activities a regulatory professional can experience.

Government Contracting

The US federal government spent approximately $29 billion on pharmaceutical research in 2008. Part of this money went to government contractors running operations centers that facilitate the conduct of the research, and these allocations are ongoing. In 1990, I was hired by Social & Scientific Systems Inc. (SSS) to work on a contract supporting the National Cancer Institute (NCI). The main task for the contractor was to authorize and make shipments of investigational new drugs to investigators participating in NCI-sponsored research. As a college student, I had worked at Becton-Dickinson doing inventory management, and the authorization of drug shipments did not seem a great leap because the principles of inventory management and tracking applied to managing clinical supplies. However, the authorization of drug shipments included a number of regulatory requirements to which I had never been exposed. For example, in order to ship drugs to a particular investigator for a particular study, the following elements had to be verified:

- The study had to be approved by NCI.
- The Investigational New Drug application (IND) had to be "open," meaning filed with the US Food and Drug Administration (FDA), have no clinical hold, be past the 30-day waiting period, etc.
- The investigator must have filed a current Form FDA-1572.
- Sufficient drug supply for the study had to be available

Additional responsibilities of this position included exposure to "expanded access studies" (programs for life-threatening diseases such as AIDS)—which fall under a set of regulations not normally encountered in the routine clinical trials process. This gave me an appreciation for the details and application of expanded access regulations.

The position with SSS exposed me to the basics as well as some unique aspects of clinical trial regulations. I was on my way to being a regulatory professional without even realizing it.

After approximately a year, I was offered a chance to work on a contract within the company for the Division of AIDS. Under this contract, my responsibilities expanded to other areas of research related to the new drug approval process—filing the IND application.

This next stage proved to be particularly challenging because I had never filed an IND. However, as many good regulatory professionals will agree, the best way to learn the subtleties of complex regulatory issues is to be a part of a well-organized and directed team with more experienced regulatory professionals. Using examples provided by SSS staff from another contract, and reading and re-reading 21 CFR 312, we crafted a "cross-referenced IND," meaning that the manufacturer allowed the Division of AIDS to have access to its IND via a letter of cross-reference. The letter was submitted to the manufacturer's IND with our new IND. The advantages in this process were twofold: the manufacturer protected trade secrets (i.e., chemistry, manufacturing and controls (CMC) information) while allowing FDA to access the necessary information, and it reduced the amount of documentation we were required to submit.

The experience on this contract, although somewhat small in comparison to other SSS contracts, was particularly rewarding because the environment was one of teambuilding and support and taught valuable lessons.

Another key regulatory task for this contract was the registration of the participating research sites. This included collecting the regulatory documents to ensure compliance with the protocol requirements and collection/verification of Form FDA-1572, research personnel resumes and CVs, and documentation of Institutional Review Board (IRB) approval and the IRB-approved informed consent form. Understanding the regulatory basis for these documents helped me grasp the integration of various regulations governing the sponsor (21 CFR 312, 612 and 812), investigator (21 CFR 312) and IRB (21 CFR 50 and 56)—collectively referred to as Good Clinical Practice (GCP).

During my tenure at SSS, I moved on to several other contracts that involved working in a regulatory support office and running two large Phase 3b studies. These opportunities allowed me to further develop my understanding of the clinical trial landscape.

Large Contract Research Organizations

Contract research organizations (CROs) provide product development services to the pharmaceutical, biotechnology and medical device industries, allowing their clients to complete these processes more efficiently and cost-effectively. Mixed reports have placed the CRO market at more than $17 billion and growing. While CROs may vary in their services and customers, regulatory services are typically included in those offered.

There were two career reasons why I switched from working for a government contractor to a CRO. The CRO environment offered the opportunity to work in product development with a focus on getting the product to market in the most expeditious manner while maintaining appropriate safeguards and regulatory documentation practices. The second reason was to expand my exposure to other therapeutic areas. My previous experience with SSS was generally restricted to life-threatening diseases and associated opportunistic infections or related *sequelae*. By moving to a CRO with many different clients, different projects and exposure to different aspects of clinical research, I got to perform many tasks both within my job description and area of expertise and outside it in a short period of time.

Independent Institutional Review Boards

An institutional review board (IRB) is an administrative body composed of scientists and nonscientists established to protect the rights and welfare of human subjects recruited to participate in research activities. An independent IRB is generally not affiliated with an institution such as an academic medical center or hospital. Rather, this standalone entity reviews research conducted at locations such as outpatient clinics and doctors' offices, or at an institution that has outsourced the review of its research. The regulations that govern IRBs in the US include 45 CFR 46 and 21 CFR 56. Additionally, under 21 CFR 312 and 812, investigators conducting research overseen by an IRB have obligations to report information to the IRB. The size of the market for independent IRBs is not easy to ascertain but there are approximately 45 independent IRBs in the US.

Prior to joining the independent IRB, I had been involved primarily with product development/clinical research on the sponsor side. A position with an independent (IRB) may seem like a huge departure from usual and customary regulatory activities, but the knowledge I had obtained working as a regulatory professional proved to be extremely beneficial in preparing me for this leadership role because of the following:

- broad regulatory knowledge
- ability to interpret regulations from multiple perspectives—IRB, sponsor, investigator
- ability to relate to clients on a regulatory level and understanding their needs and time pressures
- timelines in product development—critical milestones
- working with naive or less-experienced investigators
- code of ethics for human research

- informed consent form requirements and procedures
- ability to distinguish roles involved in research
- project management experience
- interaction with FDA
- compliance with regulations

The move to an oversight body not directly involved with the conduct of research concerned me greatly. I was worried that the regulatory knowledge I had obtained would erode over time and that my regulatory skill set would diminish, however I also thought that it would be a valuable experience. I made the effort to obtain the Regulatory Affairs Certification (RAC) in addition to obtaining the certification for IRB professionals (CIP). I continue to stay abreast of current regulatory issues by reading the applicable journals (*Regulatory Focus*, etc.) and newsletters, remaining active in RAPS and attending professional conferences and programs. What I have found is that the foundation of regulations I had learned helped me to be stronger and more effective at managing the IRB activities and staff.

Conclusion

When the opportunity presents itself, take on assignments outside traditional regulatory roles. They can give you a broader perspective on clinical research and product development as a whole, a better understanding of regulatory and an advantage in the job market. Additionally, whenever possible, contribute to the profession through presentations, training or authoring articles. Even when you are an "expert" in an area, preparation for the presentation or research for an article enhances your knowledge base as well as demonstrates your thought leadership and your willingness to contribute to the general knowledge.

CHAPTER 15

Regulatory Operations

By Katie Ditton, RAC

Regulatory operations is a regulatory subgroup that performs submission filing activities.

A regulatory operations specialist should have the FDA reviewer in mind when compiling submissions. Regulatory operations tries to ensure an easily navigable submission, so reviewers can focus on the content.

A specialist is expected to attend team meetings and work with the internal groups to finalize the submission timeline and process. It is beneficial to the process to have regulatory operations involved early to avoid the time crunch at the deadline. The other departments work long and hard on their pieces of the submission by conducting studies and authoring reports and sections of the applications. It is up to regulatory operations to finalize the submission process by seeing it through to delivery to FDA.

There are three main functions of regulatory operations: system support, publishing and document control.

System Support

Currently, there are two acceptable formats for sending submissions to FDA—paper and electronic. Paper submissions have been the traditional format but FDA has clearly stated a preference for electronic submissions.

Before electronic systems were readily available, all submissions were generated manually. It could take a regulatory operations specialist twice the time to generate the files for a submission as it does with the tools available today. Tasks included printing, hand stamping page and volume numbers, printing and attaching labels on tabs, and compiling everything by hand. Today's electronic technology makes it possible to complete this process with fewer steps and in less time.

Regulatory operations utilizes a number of systems, particularly for electronic submissions. These include document management systems (DMS), publishing systems, electronic conformity compliance checking tools and electronic submission viewing tools. In order to support regulatory operations, a system support specialist needs to understand the information technology (IT) infrastructure as well as the company's business processes. It is increasingly common for a system support specialist to have in-depth IT and/or business analyst experience, as well as, possibly, some publishing experience. A person in this role needs to be comfortable with the design and analysis of the regulatory operations business process.

The system support function involves matching end-user needs (e.g., publishing tool) and system requirements (e.g., functionality, capacity, validation concerns) to create successful submissions.

System support is heavily involved in the development lifecycle of each individual subsystem and is tasked with the selection or development, implementation, validation, maintenance and lifecycle of the systems. System support also plays a key role in evaluation of and direct liaison with system vendors, including solution implementation and daily maintenance. System support handles change requests from regulatory operations, and is expected to troubleshoot and resolve system problems.

On occasion, the system support specialist may interact with FDA (e.g., regarding specific requirements for electronic submissions, such as digital certificates).

Publishers

Publishing is required for all aspects of the product lifecycle, from premarket approval (clinical trial application submissions), to market application review and approval and, finally, to maintenance, which includes Annual Reports, postmarket commitments, labeling, advertising and promotion pieces, and safety reporting. The term "publishing" can mean anything from adjusting font in Microsoft Word documents to generating complex extensible markup language (XML) files.

The main function of a regulatory operations publisher is to create a high-quality submission in a reviewable format. The process is similar to putting a puzzle together: publishers take the submission elements authored by other departments within the organization and compile them into a cohesive submission package.

Typically, in mid-size to large companies (500–1,000 employees) regulatory affairs is responsible for the content of the submission and regulatory operations is responsible for the format (i.e., how the submission is presented). In smaller companies (under 500 employees), publishers can wear both content and formatting hats.

Large companies may also further separate the publishing function into subgroups (e.g., report publishing and submission publishing), with submission publishing sometimes further broken down into paper and electronic formats. Report publishers work solely on reports such as clinical study reports (CSRs), nonclinical reports or validation reports. Report publishers format and finalize reports so they are submission-ready.

There are two models for division of labor in publishing: project based, where a publisher is dedicated to a project(s) wherein the publisher prioritizes the work to manage every submission for that particular project; and resource pool based, where submissions are allocated to the first available publisher regardless of project.

Pre-planning to Make the Job Easier

Attention to detail is paramount in publishing. Documents need to be formatted per FDA guidance. While there is room for interpretation in some areas, others have clearly stated requirements, e.g., font size, margins and legibility. Formatting is crucial to functionality of the documents. Reviewers should be able to easily find what they need in an application. Bookmarks and links in the documents aid in the review. Ideally, publishers should be involved in formatting documents before the content is final to ensure the documents conform to the guidelines. It is also helpful to format documents before the content is final to expedite the process of compiling the documents.

Publishers often make templates for authors to use and, typically, a regulatory operations specialist would create them. Document templates are a good way of ensuring that the files authors use for the submissions are compliant with FDA guidance. Publishers can set the margins, page size, heading styles, font type, font size and page orientation in the template. They can also set the header and footer with any required information. Templates are also a good way to standardize the format within and across documents and submission and give the authors a tool to start with.

Desk procedures (i.e., not formal SOPs but a procedure that can be followed) or publishing guides and style guides (which contain information such as how the drug name should be referenced and what conventions will be used for abbreviations and reference citations) are also helpful for the regulatory operations group. It is good to have references so there is consistency across the staff and the projects when compiling a submission. The publishing guides and procedures should be considered living documents open to change as new issues are discovered or publishing decisions are made.

Regulatory operations is the last department to receive submission files before they are sent to FDA. As a result, this group is dependent upon the other departments' meeting their deadlines. Deadlines can be set by the company or come straight from the agency (i.e., review clock). If documents come in late, it can delay the submission date. This often results in extended work hours around the time the submission is due.

Publishers should be the subject matter experts in the area of submission formatting, publishing and transmission requirements. They need to attend regular project management meetings with other departments and represent the regulatory operations group. For large projects, the publisher should provide input for timelines to make sure adequate time for publishing is included in the process.

The Regulatory Submission – Common Technical Document (CTD)

In an effort to create a standard submission format across multiple regions, the International Conference on Harmonisation (ICH) created a discussion group comprising regulatory authorities from the EU, Japan and the US, and experts from the pharmaceutical industry from those regions. Regulatory authorities from other regions are observers. The ICH group created a standard format for submitting product applications called the Common Technical Document (CTD). The CTD standard was agreed upon in November 2000 and implemented in the EU, Japan and the US in July 2003.

The CTD consists of four modules. They are the Quality (Module 3; Guideline M4Q), Safety (Module 4; Guideline M4S) Efficacy (Module 5; Guideline M4E), and the Summary of all sections (Module 2) of the harmonized application. **Figure 15-1** is a diagram of the organization of the CTD. Module 1 is regional specific and is not part of the harmonized CTD.

As part of the move to electronic data exchange, the US Congress passed the *Prescription Drug User Fee Act* (*PDUFA*) in 1992. *PDUFA* authorized FDA to collect fees from companies in exchange for meeting submission review performance goals, with emphasis on tighter timelines. Included in these *PDUFA* goals were electronic data exchange and review initiatives. "FDA is committed to achieve the long-term goal of an *automated standards-based* information technology (IT) environment for the exchange, review, and management of

FIGURE 15-1. Diagrammatic Representation of the Organization of the ICH CTD Common Technical Document

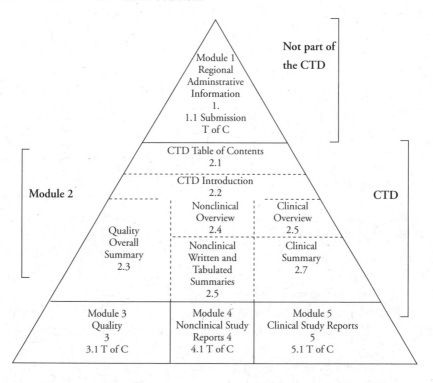

information supporting the process for the review of human drug applications throughout the *product lifecycle*."[1]

The electronic Common Technical Document (eCTD) allows for electronic transmission of the CTD. Since 1 January 2008, all electronic submissions to FDA are required to be in eCTD format. The European Medicines Agency (EMA) mandated electronic submissions as of January 2010. The eCTD specification is based on XML technology. The XML file is also known as the backbone or table of contents for the product application. The XML file follows the CTD specifications for Modules 2-5. Module 1 contains country-specific administrative information and varies by regulatory authority.

The regulatory operations specialist is required to use publishing tools, such as eCTD software, to generate eCTD submissions. Training and sometimes certification in these tools are needed. If the company submits eCTDs, the specialist must learn the eCTD validation and viewing tools.

An alternative to using a publishing system is to outsource the publishing portion of the product application. A number of services use publishing tools to generate eCTD submissions. Generally, if publishing is outsourced, the same vendor must be used for each submission (if an eCTD is filed, all subsequent amendments or supplements to that submission must also b electronic).

Standards for Electronic Submission

FDA is moving toward harmonized standards. The agency now requests compliance with Health Level Seven (HL7) standards. HL7 is an all-volunteer, not-for-profit organization involved in the development of international healthcare standards. HL7 provides standards for many different areas that are changing to electronic formats such as:

- Electronic data capture (EDC)—EDC tools automate data collection, reporting, query resolution, randomization and validation for clinical trials
- Clinical Data Interchange Standards Consortium (CDISC)—tools called Study Data Tabulation Model (SDTM) for clinical data and Standards for Exchange of Non-clinical Data (SEND) for nonclinical data
- Structured product labeling (SPL)—SPL is a standard adopted for the exchange of FDA-regulated product information including content of labeling and coding of information from the content for ease of section replacement in the future (SPL has been required for submissions with labeling since October 2005.)
- Safety reporting—MedWatch form reporting or XML format

It is helpful for regulatory operations staff to have an understanding of these initiatives so they are better positioned to assist the organization in adopting these standards.

Document Management

Document management (also known as regulatory document control) is responsible for archiving all regulatory agency documentation sent to and received from the regulatory authorities, as well as proof of delivery method. It is important to have the regulatory documentation organized and accessible in case of an FDA inspection, or for a response to the agency as illustrated by the following true story. FDA came in to inspect a company and declared it negligent in filing safety reports to the agency. The company retrieved copies of the reports and all the shipping details (including delivery receipts) from the archives, proving that FDA had received the reports, even though the agency had neglected to log them into its system. The careful maintenance of the archives saved the company from the issuance of a Form 483 or Warning Letter.

In some companies, the archivist role is performed by the publishing function and in others it is a separate function.

Document management systems (DMS) help track documents (including linking versions) and provide appropriate access to regulatory submissions. A regulatory operations specialist may help develop processes, including desk procedures (or internal process guidelines) and standard operating procedures (SOPs), on the electronic archiving of the documentation.

A specialist should be involved in determining which hard copy file system is right for the submission archives and how they should be organized. There are a number of things to consider such as access to the files, security and fireproofing. This position can also have a hand in the company's regulatory document retention policy (along with the legal department) and put processes in place to maintain files as appropriate.

This position requires some administrative activity such as copying, scanning and filing.

Fitting in With the Company and the Agency

Regulatory operations is considered a customer service function because it serves other departments within the company and is dependent upon other departments in order to complete its function. A specialist works with departments such as regulatory, Quality Assurance, quality control, manufacturing, labeling, marketing, commercial, nonclinical and clinical to provide services associated with formatting and submitting documents to the appropriate divisions within FDA.

The division at FDA with which regulatory operations interacts most often is the Office of Business Process Support (OBPS). OBPS was created in 2003 as the Information Management group. The focus at the time was to establish standards for regulatory and health data and for paper and electronic submissions. The department now also trains reviewers on the use of review tools and reports the analysis of drug review information. Regulatory operations may interact with OBPS with technical issues or formatting questions related to the submission.

If your company is sending submissions electronically, regulatory operations also may interact with FDA's Electronic Submissions Gateway (ESG) group. The ESG is a tool to transmit your submissions via the Internet. While submissions sent via CD/DVD typically take three to five days to be processed by the Central Document Control Room and made available to reviewers, submissions sent through the ESG are usually available in one day.

In addition to direct interactions with FDA, regulatory operations should proactively monitor the FDA website for changing regulations and notify the appropriate people internally when something is new or has changed. Attending FDA public hearings on topics related to submissions can also be valuable, both to receive information and provide feedback.

Educational Requirements

Work experience is the most important requirement for regulatory operations. A bachelor's degree is preferred by many companies and may be required for higher-level positions. Certifications for the electronic systems utilized by the company can be obtained directly from the system vendors. If a regulatory operations specialist functions in both a regulatory affairs role and a regulatory operations role, a background in science is required and the Regulatory Affairs Certificate (RAC) through the Regulatory Affairs Professional Society (RAPS) may be expected.

Considerations for Becoming a Specialist

Flexibility is an important quality for a specialist. As mentioned earlier, since regulatory operations is usually the last group to work on the documents, the timeline can be tight. A regulatory operations specialist needs to know when to negotiate a change to the timeline, or stand firm in order to meet a deadline.

The pace in regulatory operations can be very fast at times. A specialist will put in a lot of extra hours to make a deadline. Great attention to detail is also vital to the success of a regulatory operations specialist.

Regulatory operations is an extremely rewarding department to work in. A lot of time and effort go into a marketing application and once the product is approved, there is a great sense of accomplishment. It is a fantastic feeling to be a part of the process which moves a product to market that can potentially save lives or provide a greater quality of life to others.

References
1. Prescription Drug User Fee Act (PDUFA). FDA website. www.fda.gov/oc/pdufa/. Accessed February 2010.
2. International Conference on Harmonization website. www.ich.org/cache/compo/276-254-1.html. Accessed 20 August 2010.

Chapter 16

Regulatory Intelligence

By Linda Bowen, MS, RAC

Regulatory intelligence is a relatively new regulatory career path. It sounds very cloak and dagger, but in reality deals with public domain information. Think detective and not spy!

A dedicated regulatory intelligence group does not exist in most companies. When it is a structured function, it can range in size from one person—often a dedicated information specialist—to a large, global group aligned by therapeutic area, products, projects and/or regions.

Regardless of corporate structure, all regulatory departments conduct regulatory intelligence and anyone working in regulatory has performed one or more regulatory intelligence activities during his or her career. At a minimum, this entails keeping up-to-date on the latest regulatory and perhaps even legislative developments.

So what is regulatory intelligence? The Drug Information Association Regulatory Affairs Special Interest Area Community—Regulatory Intelligence Working Group has defined it as:

> "...the act of gathering and analyzing publicly available regulatory information. This includes communicating the implications of that information, and monitoring the current regulatory environment for opportunities to shape future regulations, guidance, policy, and legislation."

Although the "art" of regulatory intelligence has been around as long as the health authorities have been approving products, it has grown in scope and importance within the last 10 years due to the availability of online information (the Internet) and increased transparency by government entities. Regulatory intelligence is important to organizations and project teams because it can help guide them in FDA's current thinking on specific issues, provide more detail about studies that are required for approval of certain types of products, and can provide valuable information that can be used by the commercial organization to predict approval dates and indications for competitors.

General Qualifications for Specializing in This Area

With the growing specializations available to regulatory professionals, a need arose for generalists to be available to answer questions and provide advice across regions, topics and therapeutic areas. The growth of specialization areas coincided with the birth of the dedicated regulatory intelligence group.

Depending upon the products your company markets, a degree with a specialty in the life sciences, engineering or pharmacy would provide a good background for a career in regulatory intelligence. If you plan to be more involved on the policy end, a degree in law or political science might be helpful. Other desirable skills and experience include:

- five or more years of regulatory affairs experience
- general knowledge of regulatory processes
- analytical thinking
- excellent communication and presentation skills
- networking skills
- negotiation and influencing skills
- prior interactions with health authorities
- information junkie
- fortune teller

The last bullet point was added because we are often called upon to help predict what will happen based upon past precedent and current trends.

Most people working in the regulatory intelligence function come from a regulatory, clinical or medical background. It is important to understand how the health authorities work, so prior regulatory experience is a definite plus. In particular, a regulatory generalist background, gained by working in a small group with exposure to different areas within regulatory (chemistry, manufacturing and controls (CMC), labeling, advertising, operations), would be beneficial to a person wishing to work in a regulatory intelligence group.

Experience across different therapeutic product types such as drugs (over-the-counter, prescription, generic), biologics, medical devices and combination products is a must. Diversification in the pharmaceutical industry can happen overnight; what you are responsible for today could change tomorrow.

Specialized Areas in Regulatory Intelligence
Countries or Regions

Regulatory intelligence is closely aligned and "intertwined" with regulatory policy, government relations, public policy and state relations. These last four functions differ greatly from organization to organization but are the groups with their fingers on the pulse of legislative matters.

Individuals supporting countries or regions have a breadth of general knowledge about those areas and are knowledgeable about all facets of the government, not just the health authorities.

Operations

Are you a computer whiz who has regulatory aspirations but no regulatory experience? The people in this group support the computer-based functions of the regulatory intelligence group. This can include a group intranet site, a newsletter, database development and maintenance, shared drives, etc.

Therapeutic Domains

Individuals who support a therapeutic area or specific disease must keep abreast of competitor products, both in development and postmarketing. They should have a good understanding of the diseases in their domains, including the standard of treatment in the markets they cover. This group collects information on submission strategies and bases for approval (precedents).

Topics

Global experts on specific regulatory topics; these topics could include registration requirements, compliance issues, electronic submissions, pediatrics, data protection, exclusivity provisions, CMC requirements or even a more general topic such as biologics or medical devices.

Services Within the Regulatory Intelligence Department

The regulatory intelligence group helps the company better understand new or revised regulations, guidances and/or policies or other significant regulatory developments, including trends—and the impact they may have on the company. It influences the regulatory environment by building relationships with trade and professional organizations. Members of the regulatory intelligence group are the drivers of the commenting and consultation process—maintaining one "regulatory voice" from the company; they maintain lists of regulatory experts and key opinion leaders.

Surveillance, Analysis and Impact

Among the most important functions in regulatory intelligence are surveillance and analysis. It is crucial that newly published or revised regulations and/or guidelines, which have the potential to directly impact a company's drug development and lifecycle management, be analyzed and their impact communicated to management. Metrics and trends are also important, especially on review cycles and approval times. Some regulatory intelligence groups also provide monthly and yearly reports summarizing the activities in their regions or therapeutic areas.

The surveillance function can feed information to a newsletter to a predetermined distribution list; to a database supporting knowledge management; or to a project team that needs to stay current regarding the regulatory, legislative and competitive landscape to support development and/or lifecycle management of their products.

This process can be time consuming and the cause of information overload, but is an absolute necessity in order for a regulatory group to conduct daily business.

There are subscription regulatory databases available to assist in daily global surveillance.

Search Activities

Usually conducted on an *ad hoc* basis to support regulatory development or lifecycle management strategies, the search function is the most challenging and time consuming of all the activities that a regulatory intelligence group conducts. Here are some typical searches:

- A search for regulatory precedents for a competitive product, which could seek to answer the following questions:
    o What regulatory pathway did the competitor use to get the product approved?
    o Who were the agency reviewers?
    o Was there a specific regulation or guidance to support approval?
    o What is the review division's track record?
    o Was this inactive ingredient ever used in an approved, injectable product?
    o How many clinical trials were needed?

- o What comparators were used?
- o How many other drugs have been approved with the same indication?
- o Did competitive products have other indications approved?
- A search for a specific regulation, guidance or policy to support development
- A search for trends (review cycles, approval times, expanded access, etc.) to provide metrics on competitors' products

Driving the Commenting/Consultation Process

When a draft or revised regulation or guidance is published, it often is in the best interest of the company to provide feedback to the issuing health authority. The coordination of the commenting/consultation process is driven by the regulatory intelligence group. This ensures a single opinion or "one regulatory voice" from the company.

Participation in Due Diligence Teams

In this ever-evolving world, the regulatory intelligence function has become an integral part of in-licensing and due diligence activities. The group must become efficient at putting together information packages for this activity, usually on a moment's notice, to support the actual due diligence exercise. These data can include information on products, competitors, strategies used, past employees, compliance issues, etc.

Conclusion

If you are looking for a challenge in the regulatory world, regulatory intelligence is the career path for you. The evolving legislative and regulatory landscape will keep you on your toes. And I promise you will never get bored.

CHAPTER 17

Your Career as a Biopharmaceutical Regulatory Writer

By Nancy R. Katz, PhD

One option for a career in regulatory affairs is becoming a regulatory writer in the biopharmaceutical industry. This profession is acknowledged as meaningful and challenging, and regulatory writers are recognized as vital to the industry. Regulatory writers are employed in biotechnology, pharmaceutical and medical device companies, as well as contract research organizations (CROs), and can be full-time staff members or consultants to all of the above. This chapter describes the work of a regulatory writer in the field of drug research. It explains the fundamental knowledge required to perform the work and the specialized knowledge needed for success. Its focus is on submission of drug applications in the US.

What do Regulatory Writers Write?

Regulatory writers in the biopharmaceutical industry create documents, such as protocols and data summaries, for submission to regulatory agencies in support of drug development. Specifically, they create documents compliant with the requirements of the Common Technical Document (CTD), a set of specifications governing applications in support of new medicinal products. The CTD was developed by the International Conference on Harmonisation (ICH). Consisting of representatives from three regions,—the US, the EU and Japan—ICH develops common standards and practices related to the process of drug development and registration. Such practices are intended to "reduce or obviate the need to duplicate the testing carried out during the research and development of new medicines." ICH developed the CTD in order to decrease the time and resources needed to compile and review a drug application as well as to simplify the exchange of information among regulatory authorities.[1] The CTD, particularly now that is usually submitted electronically (an "eCTD"), has become the *raison d'être* for regulatory writers.

Who Are Regulatory Writers?

Regulatory writers come from a variety of backgrounds. Currently, no clearly defined degree or certification is required for someone to be hired as a regulatory writer. However, almost all those employed in the industry hold at least a bachelor's degree; very often, they have an advanced degree, such as a master's or doctorate, or a professional degree such as an RN, JD, MD or PharmD. While many regulatory writers have scientific backgrounds, a significant number with liberal arts training are highly successful regulatory writers. Regardless of their education and background, successful regulatory writers understand the process of drug development and are thoroughly conversant with the CTD structure and guidelines.

The Fundamentals—Understanding Drug Development and the CTD
Drug Development in a Nutshell

A regulatory writer needs to understand enough about drug development to determine which documents need to be written. The decision to create a particular document is based upon the drug's stage of development and the region of the world in which that document will be submitted. The goal of research in the biopharmaceutical industry is to bring to market a product that fulfills an unmet medical need. A pharmaceutical or biotechnology company that sponsors the development of a drug (the sponsor) must determine whether that drug will be a viable medicinal therapy. That is, the sponsor must find out whether that drug is effective in a certain indication (disease or condition, such as asthma or obesity) and whether the benefits of that drug outweigh its risks—often called adverse effects. The sponsor first tests the drug *in vitro*—"in glass"—and then *in vivo*—in animals, usually mice, rats, dogs, rabbits and sometimes monkeys and other primates. If data from these investigations are encouraging, a US sponsor submits an application known as an Investigational New Drug Application (IND) to FDA. Technically, the IND is a formal request to ship the drug across state lines; in fact, the IND is a petition to test the drug in human subjects. After review of the application, FDA will authorize studies of the drug in human subjects if it believes that participation in these studies does not expose subjects to unreasonable risks. An independent ethics committee also reviews the clinical study protocol associated with the IND for the same reason. In the US, this group is called an institutional review board (IRB); in Europe and many other regions of the world, it is known as an ethics committee (EC).

Investigations of a new drug intended for use in human subjects consist of three phases of clinical trials. If data from these trials are encouraging, a US sponsor submits a formal application, known as a New Drug Application (NDA), to FDA asking that the drug be approved for marketing and sales. If the drug is a vaccine or a blood product, the sponsor submits a Biological License Application (BLA). If, after review, FDA deems the drug to be effective and safe when used as directed, it will approve the drug for marketing. Very likely, it will require the sponsor to conduct more studies in human subjects in order to determine how the drug affects large segments of the population.

Submitting a drug application such as an IND, NDA or BLA (also known as the "dossier," the "filing" and the "submission") is a mandatory process for any sponsor who wants to sell and market a drug in the US. The application must be based on the CTD described earlier. The process of compiling a CTD-compliant application is time consuming and labor intensive. More often than not, the scientists and clinicians who have worked to develop a drug do not have the time, resources or skills to write the individual documents contained in any of these applications. Thus, the stage is set for the regulatory writer. A writer who understands the regulations governing both drug development and the CTD—the basis of the IND, NDA or BLA—and who has the skills and dedication necessary to create these documents becomes an invaluable partner to those in the field of drug development.

The CTD in a Nutshell

The CTD consists of five sections, referred to as modules. The five modules are described below, along with some of the documents required for each. (Note on nomenclature: Writers who write documents for Modules 3 and 4 are often called technical writers. Those who write documents for Module 5 are often called medical writers. Both types of writers are properly called regulatory writers.)

Module 1: Regional Administrative Information

This module is not considered part of the CTD proper because it contains regional documents, many of an administrative nature, that are not "common" to all regions (the US, the EU or Japan). Rather, the documents in this module are specific to the region in which the drug is being submitted. Because regulatory

writers are often involved in creating documents contained in this module, some key Module 1 documents are listed below:
- general investigational plan
- risk management plans
- product label (often called the "package insert")
- Investigator's Brochure (This document is prepared for the investigator who conducts a clinical trial. It presents current nonclinical and clinical data about the drug under investigation as well as a description of the drug's active and inactive ingredients.)

Module 2: Summaries

This module consists of high-level summaries of information found in Modules 3, 4 and 5. Documents contained in Module 2 include:
- quality overall summary, which includes subsections for materials, validations, analytical procedures and stability
- nonclinical overview, which provides conclusions about nonclinical investigations
- nonclinical summaries—both written and tabulated—of *in vitro* studies and *in vivo* pharmacodynamic, pharmacokinetic, toxicology and immunologic studies in animals
- clinical overview, which provides conclusions about clinical investigations and includes an analysis of the risks and benefits of the drug to human subjects
- clinical summaries—both written and tabulated—of bioanalytical methods and of pharmacokinetic, pharmacodynamic, immunologic, efficacy and safety studies in human subjects

Module 3: Quality

This module contains the chemistry, manufacturing and controls (CMC) information. It consists of reports (and associated study protocols and protocol amendments) conducted to characterize the pharmaceutical nature of the drug and ensure its purity (quality).

Module 4: Safety

This module contains reports, associated study protocols and protocol amendments for *in vitro* studies and *in vivo* studies—pharmacokinetic, pharmacodynamic, toxicologic and immunologic—of the drug in animals.

Module 5: Efficacy

This module contains reports, associated study protocols and protocol amendments for studies of the drug in human subjects. Included in this section are the reports of pharmacokinetic, pharmacodynamic, toxicologic and immunologic studies as well as the following types of studies:

- Phase 1, 2 and 3 clinical studies, which include narrative summaries detailing how the drug has affected individual patients
- Integrated Summary of Safety (ISS) and Integrated Summary of Efficacy (ISE)—although these documents are entitled "summaries," they actually contain analyses of pooled data; thus, they differ from the nonclinical and clinical summaries found in Module 2
- Postmarket reports

Other Required Skills and How to Acquire Them

Following are additional areas of knowledge as well as specific skill sets that can play a role in a successful career in regulatory writing. If the list appears daunting, be encouraged by the fact that successful and seasoned regulatory writers are mere mortals who have managed to learn these subjects.

Regulations

Learn the relevant regional, national and local regulations governing drug development. If you are writing documents in support of drugs that will be tested and/or filed for marketing in the US, become familiar with the following parts of volume 21 of the Code of Federal Regulations (21 CFR):

- 11: Electronic Submissions and Signatures
- 50: Specifications for Protection of Human Subjects in Clinical Trials
- 56: Specifications for Institutional Review Boards That Oversee Clinical Trials
- 58: Description of Good Laboratory Practices for Nonclinical Studies Associated With Clinical Trials
- 312: Requirements for an Investigational New Drug
- 314: Requirements for Applications for Approval and Marketing of a New Drug

Be aware of four key ICH guidelines regarding the conduct and reporting of a clinical trial:

- *Clinical Data Safety Management: Definitions and Standards for Expedited Reporting E2A*
- *Structure and Content of Clinical Study Reports E3*

- *Guideline for Good Clinical Practice E6*
- *General Considerations for Clinical Trials E8*

Become familiar with four key ICH guidelines regarding the CTD as well as the overall CTD table of contents:
- *Organization of the Common Technical Document for the Registration of Pharmaceuticals for Human Use M4*
- *The Common Technical Document for the Registration of Pharmaceuticals for Human Use: Quality—M4Q(R1) Quality Overall Summary of Module 2; Module 3: Quality*
- *The Common Technical Document for the Registration of Pharmaceuticals for Human Use: Safety—M4S(R2) Nonclinical Overview and Nonclinical Summaries of Module 2; Organization of Module 4*
- *The Common Technical Document for the Registration of Pharmaceuticals for Human Use: Efficacy—M4E(R1) Clinical Overview and Clinical Summary of Module 2; Module 5: Clinical Study Reports*

Understand the principles embodied in the *US Health Insurance Portability and Accountability Act* (*HIPAA*) and the Declaration of Helsinki. The former ensures the privacy of data related to healthcare. The latter is the declaration of the World Medical Association regarding ethical conduct of research in human subjects. Cornerstone principles of this declaration are the right of individuals to self-determination and to make informed decisions. This declaration is considered by many to be morally binding.

Data and How to Work With Them

Learn basic principles of the following:
- biostatistics
- programming
- data entry
- data interpretation
- coding of adverse events and drugs via specialized dictionaries such as the *Medical Dictionary for Regulatory Activities* (*MedDRA*) and the World Health Organization (WHO) drug dictionary

Drug Characterization and Mechanism of Action

Learn the basics of the following:
- chemistry, manufacture and control of the drug, including the drug substance and the final drug product

- pharmacology of the drug, including its pharmacokinetics and pharmacodynamics (that is, what the body does to the drug and what the drug does to the body)

○○Principles and Practices of Clinical Trials
Be conversant with the following:
- protocol design, both nonclinical and clinical, including the logistics of the proposed trials
- safety reporting, including the reporting of serious adverse events
- creation of the final study report for a clinical trial
- basic clinical laboratory tests and interpretation of chest X-rays and electrocardiograms (ECGs)

Diseases and Conditions

Gain a working knowledge of the following for the drug on which you are writing:
- etiology of the targeted indication (disease or condition, such as asthma, multiple sclerosis, diabetes, obesity and infections caused by Gram-negative or Gram-positive pathogens resistant to current antibiotics)
- current treatments for the indication or condition and reasons why the drug may fulfill an unmet medical need
- immunologic responses of the body to the drug in healthy individual and individuals with the proposed condition for treatment

Care and Feeding of Documents

FDA strongly encourages electronic submission of CTD-based drug applications (eCTDs), whether INDs, NDAs or BLAs. Electronic submissions enable all documents contained in the application to be linked electronically to one another by means of an XML backbone—the technological core of the CTD. Linking allows reviewers to conduct online reviews of the application and facilitates traceability of information and data. Therefore, it is necessary for the regulatory writer to understand electronic documents and to have a command of the following:
- basic and advanced computing skills with the following programs and formats:
    o Microsoft Word, including the Styles feature
    o Microsoft PowerPoint, Microsoft Excel and Adobe Acrobat
    o Creation and format of tables (in Microsoft Word), figures

(in Prism or other graphing software) and study schemas (in Microsoft Visio or other software)
- use of templates, including links within and between documents
- preparation of a document for linking to an XML backbone
- methods of archiving and referencing documents

Art and Craft of Writing
Be skilled in the following:
- basic writing, including a firm command of organization, syntax, grammar, punctuation and logical development of information
- document style
    - standard style guides such as the *AMA Manual of Style, 10th edition* and the *Chicago Manual of Style*
    - in-house style of the sponsor for whom you write—usually a combination of one of the manuals mentioned above and sponsor idiosyncrasies

Business Acumen
Be knowledgeable about the following:
- The business of your business—how the drug you are writing about fits into the worldwide market of drug products
- The politics and goals of the organization in which you are working
- Basic business skills—project management, estimating time and costs for projects, writing contracts
- Procedures for reviewing and signing off documents

How Do I Learn all of This?
You learn by a combination of the following: doing; absorbing the counsel of a willing mentor (see below on what a mentor is and how to find one); taking courses in the field; and independent reading and research. You also create a development plan so you can assess and then fill in the gaps in your knowledge.

Just Do It!
The best way to learn is by doing. Given an assignment, plunge in—intelligently. Look for an approved example of the document you are assigned to write as well as any regulations, both draft and final, governing the creation

of that document. Then perform a bit of reverse engineering. For example, if you are assigned to write a clinical study report (CSR), obtain the ICH E3 Guidelines (mentioned above), the study protocol, tables, listings, figures and in-house style guide. Then examine the report section by section and figure out how the writer of the approved document created that document.

One-on-one Mentoring

Find the right mentor, and life can be close to blissful. In Homer's *Odyssey*, Mentor was the wise and trusted counselor of Telemachus, son of Odysseus. Athena, goddess of wisdom, sometimes assumed the guise of Mentor in order to counsel Telemachus. Your mentor will probably not be Athena or come to you unasked. But you can ask a person inside or outside your organization to mentor you. That person should be well versed in some aspect of drug development—possibly a regulatory writer, clinical research associate (CRA), biostatistician, regulatory affairs associate or research scientist. That person should also be willing and able to share the benefit of his or her experience with you and, if appropriate, provide you with constructive feedback about your work. The mentoring relationship entails a commitment of time and energy on the part of both individuals. Honor it by heeding the advice of your mentor, asking your mentor for feedback about your work (if appropriate) and preparing thoughtful questions about issues related to daily tasks, corporate policies and regulations governing drug development.

Coursework

Industry-sponsored courses that describe the processes and regulations associated with drug development abound. The Drug Information Association (DIA), Regulatory Affairs Professionals Society (RAPS) and American Medical Writers Association (AMWA) offer coursework leading to certification in many aspects of drug development. AMWA also offers courses that teach individuals how to write for a scientific and regulatory audience. The Pharmaceutical Education Research Institute (PERI) sponsors courses explaining the biological basis of specific indications and optimal ways to conduct clinical trials with drugs targeting that indication.

University-sponsored courses also exist. The University of Chicago and the University of the Sciences in Philadelphia sponsor programs that lead to certification in medical writing; the latter also offers a master's degree program in medical writing.

Independent Reading: Print and Online

Many resources exist that will enable you to further your training in regulatory writing on your own. Some of these are listed below. Many of the books in print are issued with CDs or allow access to an online version of the material.

STYLE AND FORMATTING GUIDES
- *AMA Manual of Style, 10th edition*
- *Scientific Style and Format: The CSE Manual for Authors, Editors, and Publisher, 7th edition*
- *Microsoft Word for Medical and Technical Writers* by Peter G. Aitken and Maxine M. Okazaki

GUIDES TO REGULATORY WRITING
- *Targeted Regulatory Writing Techniques: Clinical Documents for Drugs and Biologics* by Linda Fossati Wood and MaryAnn Foote

REFERENCE BOOKS
- *The Merck Manual* (physician and home editions)
- *Pharmacokinetics Made Easy* by Donald J. Birkett
- *Medical Abbreviations: 30,000 Conveniences at the Expense of Communication and Safety, 14th edition* by Neil M. Davis
- *A Manual of Laboratory & Diagnostic Tests* by Frances Talaska Fischbach
- *How to Report Statistics in Medicine, 2nd edition* by Thomas A. Lang and Michelle Secic
- *Fundamentals of US Regulatory Affairs, 6th edition*
- *Stedman's Medical Dictionary*
- *Mosby's 2010 Nursing Drug Reference* by Linda Skidmore-Roth.
- *Guide to Clinical Trials* by Bert Spilker

MAGAZINES AND JOURNALS
- *Applied Clinical Trials* (trade journal)
- DIA publications, especially *DIA Today*

Anything Else I Need to Know?

There are two more fundamentals for success in this area.

You must get along with people and work as part of a team. A regulatory writer does not work alone. To create clearly written documents that comply with the regulations, contain accurate statements about the data they present and are internally consistent, you must interact successfully with other people. For instance, you will need to obtain data and other information from people in all parts of the organization you work in; work with others to craft interpretations of the data (often called "messages"); circulate documents for review; address and adjudicate comments from colleagues; and finalize documents for publication in electronic format. After a review of one of your documents, you may have to re-conceptualize it completely and rewrite it from the ground up. Your success in these areas depends upon your ability and willingness to subordinate your ego when necessary and to assert yourself when appropriate. If doing this does not come naturally to you, many courses sponsored under the catch-all terms "leadership" and "management" can teach you how to work and play with your colleagues. Interpersonal skills are serious skills and their lack can compromise your career as a regulatory writer.

You must continue training—and have a development plan. That is, you must continually reassess your skill sets and knowledge base, identify gaps that can impede your ability to function as a regulatory writer and figure out how to plug those gaps. The world of drug development is never static, and in this fast-paced environment, you must, to quote Carl Sagan, "learn how to learn."

Summary

Your work as a regulatory writer helps bring medicines that potentially improve quality of life, alleviate suffering and cure disease to the people who need them. As a regulatory writer, you will work with the brightest and the best of research and clinical scientists to accurately and meticulously report research results in a manner that facilitates review by a regulatory agency. To succeed in this career, you must understand the basics of drug development, the regulations that govern this process, and the rationale and structure of the CTD. Above all, you must get along with people, work as part of a team and constantly reassess the skills needed to write the documents you are asked to write. Drug development, including the rules and procedures that govern it, is here to stay. And so are regulatory writers.

References
1. US Food and Drug Administration (FDA), Center for Drug Evaluation and Research, *Guidance for Industry M4: Organization of the CTD*).

CHAPTER 18

How I Got Into Regulatory

By Christine Conroy

It all started in pharmacy school in the mid-1980s when a package insert was a novel thing to me. I remember thinking, "Wow, what a great job it would be to write one of these!" But, at that time, I had no idea how the pharmaceutical industry operated and I certainly had no idea there was such a thing as a regulatory career. This was also a time when pharmacy students were generally discouraged from careers in industry and the opportunities afforded by industry were little appreciated. Nevertheless, I found myself continuing to be intrigued by what industry might offer. This feeling was only enhanced by my participation in a school program that Eli Lilly and Company offered for the purpose of teaching students about the pharmaceutical industry.

An initial impediment to my pursuing a career in industry was that I lived in Colorado and was not prepared to move to the East Coast or the West Coast where the regulatory jobs are most available. So, I shelved thoughts of working in industry and practiced pharmacy for a few years. One thing led to another and before long I found myself living in Northern California and presented with an opportunity to work as a drug information pharmacist for Syntex Laboratories Inc. The department I worked in was a predecessor to modern-day medical affairs and a dynamic environment to say the least. This experience was wonderfully rich because Syntex's Naprosyn (naproxen) was the king of nonsteroidal anti-inflammatory drugs (although being challenged by competitors) and a number of other promising compounds were in late stage development or under active FDA review. Over the next several years, five new Syntex compounds, all in different therapeutic areas, were approved and launched. Because of the activities surrounding the marketing of Naprosyn as well as approval and launch of several new products, I was able to observe and participate in all kinds of regulatory activities. However, initially I lacked an understanding of what it was all about.

My cluelessness can be summed up by an incident soon after joining Syntex: I kept hearing people say with great force and conviction that Dee Dee Mack said that certain promotional activities were fine but others were not. I assumed they were talking about a very powerful woman at FDA and often thought to myself, "Wow, I wonder who she is, I'd really like to meet her." Well, it was not long before I learned, much to my chagrin, that Dee Dee Mack was, in fact, not a powerful woman at FDA but rather the acronym DDMAC, which stood for the Division of Drug Marketing, Advertising and Communication!

It was quite some time before I was willing to admit my "misunderstanding" to anyone, but because of interactions with my regulatory colleagues during this time my interest in and aptitude for regulatory became apparent. As is often the case, change presents opportunity. In the mid-1990s, Hoffmann-LaRoche bought Syntex and during the period of transition I took what I thought was a temporary position in regulatory to help transfer files in conjunction with closing the Syntex development site in Palo Alto. In the end, the site closure was postponed and I worked for Roche Global Development as the regulatory representative on global project teams for about five more years. During this time, I had the opportunity to work on large projects and participate in regulatory activities in the US and Europe, including many unique activities such as an advisory committee meeting in the US and a Committee for Human Pharmaceuticals (CHMP, formerly CPMP) oral hearing in Europe.

In late 2001, Roche did close the main development site in Palo Alto and I was faced with a decision whether to stay with Roche and move to a different location or to change companies and stay in California. I ultimately decided it was time to try life in a small biotechnology company, so opted for the latter. I joined a company called Genitope Inc., and worked on a novel patient-specific vaccine for non-Hodgkins lymphoma. The change from a large pharmaceutical company to a small biotechnology firm initially was a real shock and the transition from having a multitude of resources at my fingertips to just having to figure things out was difficult. Issues and challenges that I had never even considered presented themselves daily. After about six months, I settled into my new life and began to enjoy participating in the diverse activities required for a company to transition from an academic orientation to full clinical development.

I learned a great deal in the nearly three years I spent at Genitope, but when an opportunity presented itself at another small company where I could establish the regulatory function, I decided it was time to try to fly on my own. I made the move to Affymax in late 2004, a time when the company had about 50 employees and was just starting clinical development of its lead compound, Hematide. Life at Affymax has been rewarding, as the compound is now in Phase 3 clinical development and I have been able and fortunate to grow with the company and make the transition from being a member of the regulatory department as a senior director when I started to currently leading a group as vice president, regulatory affairs and GCP compliance.

Chapter 19

How I Got Started in Regulatory

By Evangeline D. Loh, PhD, RAC

Life is serendipity. I certainly did not matriculate at Cornell thinking I wanted to be in regulatory. I wanted to make a difference. In fact, like many students, I was lured to science as an undergraduate major because it would be an appropriate platform for medical school. I spent two summers as an intern at a biotechnology company where I had some fascinating research projects. One and a half years later, in the midst of fulfilling my bachelor's in microbiology requirements, I realized that I was not passionate about being a physician. Research was a possibility. I was involved in some animal nutrition research that I enjoyed, and I liked reading and reviewing the associated scientific research articles. However, I would not be serving the community. I was enamored of an upper-level elective class in business law, particularly leveraging precedence and case law in the written essay questions. I was also engaged in numerous extracurricular activities that permitted development of leadership and organizational skills. These experiences contributed greatly to important professional skills: leadership, teamwork, management, public speaking and event organization. It also made me appreciate the importance of a balanced education, but I had to make a choice of what to do for my future. After much consideration, I decided that above all things, I enjoyed science and research; so I decided to pursue graduate education as the next step. I was accepted into the PhD program in pharmacology at the University of Texas Health Science Center in San Antonio.

It was there that I decided that research was not my primary interest. I certainly appreciated the intellectual pursuit of science and the methodical and logical approach to research. I honed seminal skills such as searching the scientific literature as well as writing technical materials. Once again, I chose to be involved in different activities that required development of important professional skills. My experience in graduate school was fairly traumatizing and at this point not worth wasting ink to describe. My thesis followed a research approach given the moniker "reverse molecular pharmacology." I did graduate, I was able to publish, I learned a lot and I appreciated the challenges of graduate students.

Once again serendipity came into play in the form of an opportunity available at the Association of American Medical Schools (AAMS) for an individual in graduate education and science policy. This was a perfect way to impact graduate education policy, about which I felt strongly. Not to wax philosophical, but the apprenticeship and indentured servitude model was unfair and I wanted to change it.

I chose to enroll in a course from the School of Nursing at Georgetown University (Barnett/Parexel) entitled, "Developing Skills as a Clinical Research Associate," as clinical research skills seemed to be in demand. This course furthered my interest in human clinical research. At the AAMC, I was exposed to many opportunities to be involved in graduate education as well as clinical research policy. We were slowly reforming academic medicine. The position required dealing with different clients: graduate students, postdoctoral fellows, graduate school deans and clinical researchers. I managed a few different groups, including a task force of medical school clinical research deans and industry representatives from the Pharmaceutical Research and Manufacturers Association (PhRMA) who sought to investigate industry-sponsored clinical trials in academic settings. It was through this task force that I learned about clinical research and protecting human patients. The concept of "therapeutic misconception" was pivotal: there is a difference between clinical research/clinical trials and standard clinical care. We published a paper on the use of central institutional review boards (IRBs), and I realized how much I enjoyed reviewing regulations and writing about them. I researched regulatory affairs and spoke to some family friends who were in the industry.

Once again, serendipity struck: an opportunity arose as a regulatory affairs scientist at Cook Medical, a device development company. I had all the science skills and only required some formal exposure to regulatory affairs. I was fortunate to be given the opportunity at Cook Medical.

I had the luxury of being involved with many different types of devices at Cook Medical. I focused mostly on US and EU regulations, but since there was a global business strategy, I also got to be involved in global regulatory strategy, and became familiar with other markets: South Korea, Japan and Hong Kong. Early in my tenure, I attended a Food and Drug Law Institute (FDLI) training on medical devices, which presented the regulations from a lawyer's perspective. Also, I read voraciously about US and EU medical device regulations as well as those of other countries. Cook offered training and I attended every webinar, even if it meant working late to participate or skipping lunch. I capitalized on all the training opportunities.

As a regulatory scientist, I was assigned to participate in product development teams involving engineering, regulatory, marketing and sales. One of the most educational products was a device with an ancillary medicinal product. I asked to participate on device projects I felt were interesting or that would develop a particular expertise. I also obviously compiled and submitted regulatory submissions.

I studied and took both the RAPS US and EU RAC exams, and earned these certifications. There are not many ways in the industry to demonstrate regulatory competence, but the RAC designation is one mechanism.

I also became aware of many of my own preferences while at Cook. I loved reading the regulations, and while I did not have the legal training, I had enough background and ability to research and common sense to understand what was not explicit. Regulations and laws are subject to interpretation, but there is also much guidance. It is critical to document one's position and provide a rationale. Also, the Internet has made information much more accessible.

Some time later, Emergo, a device contract research organization, advertised for a director of regulatory affairs. I thought this was the perfect opportunity to deal with multiple clients with different medical devices in different markets in the world. Also, this position was an amalgamation of regulatory affairs and customer service/association activities and policy. It was particularly enticing that Emergo was committed to certain values: customer satisfaction and responsiveness, integrity and high service standards. Emergo, like many employers, indicated that the RAC designation was a plus and wanted an individual who could communicate well and was poised and professional.

One of Emergo's business models is to serve as a local representative in foreign markets on behalf of device makers. As vice president of regulatory affairs, I manage our clients and activities for the European and Australian markets. Emergo is often engaged to perform regulatory strategy assessments as well as compile regulatory documents. At Emergo, I have been given the opportunity to manage many different projects as well as groups of clients. I have also been writing for different trade publications, which has been a surprisingly creative outlet.

Regulatory is the exciting interface between science, regulations and logic. Good communication skills are essential. By enabling a device to be marketed in many countries and regions of the world, one makes a difference in healthcare. It is also exciting to note that while differences in medical device regulations remain, there are also similarities and the activities of harmonization groups are diminishing some of those differences. It is neat to evaluate the different regulatory models and consider from a policy perspective how they encourage innovation or hinder advancement. For example, are there ethical ramifications to preventing patients' access to novel medical devices or is this just the regulatory authorities' mandate to protect patient safety? It is a fine line. A regulatory professional needs to stay informed about the current regulations and requirements and preparation is essential.

That said, while serendipity is certainly a theme in my career as a regulatory affairs professional, a certain amount of preparation was required. This Louis Pasteur quote is very apropos: "Chance favors the prepared mind."

How to Prepare for Regulatory as a Career

Familiarize yourself with the regulatory profession. Spend time on the RAPS website. There are some outstanding career resources available.

Demonstrate interest in regulatory if you are not currently in a position that offers opportunities to be more involved in regulatory activities. Enroll in courses, participate in webinars, read material. Many employees are able to transition into regulatory by speaking with the department and informing HR of their interest.

If you have the luxury to enroll in a graduate program in regulatory, there are many programs now available that offer formal training.

It is vital that regulatory professionals communicate well. Thus, regulatory professionals should write as well as speak eloquently. Hone your technical writing skills by taking courses and practicing, and get involved in organizations such as Toastmasters that allow you to practice your speaking abilities. Also, participate in organizations and committees where you can express your opinion and contribute to the team.

If you are in regulatory, prepare, study and take one or more of the Regulatory Affairs Certification (RAC) exams (US, Canada, EU and General Scope). Studying for the RAC actually provides great background. The certification demonstrates your competency and commitment to the industry.

Regulatory requires constant reading. Regulations and guidance are frequently changing. This makes the field interesting.

Chapter 20

How I Got Started in Regulatory

By Meredith Brown-Tuttle, RAC

Like most of us in regulatory, I came to this career by a circuitous route. After graduating from college with a degree in biological psychology, I saw several options open to me:
- research assistant
- market researcher
- clinical researcher
- scientific writer
- master's degree student

I wrote several different resumes to accommodate all of the above career choices, but I really wanted to focus on getting into clinical research, I felt this would best combine my biology background, outgoing personality and organizational skills. After five months of sending out my resume, going on countless interviews and experiencing my fair share of frustration, I was offered two different jobs at the same time: regulatory associate doing clinical and regulatory or data management at a pharmaceutical company. Which did I choose? I chose data management, of course. Why? I love regulatory; in fact I wear the moniker of "regulatory geek" with pride and yet I went away from that path at the beginning because I did not know any better.

Reflecting on my past, I would not have done it any differently. In college, as a research assistant, I filled out institutional review board (IRB) forms, created case report forms (CRFs), ran subjects through experiments, collected data, analyzed data and wrote up the results. Data management felt more comfortable to me at that time. As a data management coordinator, I wrote edit checks, built databases, learned how to assure database quality, interact with clients and manage outstanding issues, and created CRFs based on a protocol. After a year, I realized I really wanted to get closer to the action and become a clinical research associate (CRA). I did find a job as a CRA and ended up running a multicenter trial, including monitoring, setting up investigator studies and the database and managing the data entry personnel. This work built upon my skills from my previous job.

At this point, I realized that I needed more education. The University of California, Santa Cruz, had just started a Clinical Trial Design and Management certificate program and I enrolled. During this time, I decided to try my hand at full-time medical writing since I had written white papers, applications and abstracts as a CRA. I found that I loved writing full time. When I took my last class at UC Santa Cruz, in domestic and international regulatory affairs I realized that regulatory combined my skills in project management, data analysis and clinical and medical writing. In four years I had changed job functions four times because I was exploring my career and finding out what worked for me—and everything I learned ultimately helped me get hired when I sent out my resume for an entry-level position in regulatory. In June 2000, I started in regulatory and have not thought about changing jobs since.

CHAPTER 21

Paving the Way to a Regulatory Career—How I Got Started

By Stephanie Anderson

Almost a year into a master's degree program, I forced myself to sit down and decide what to do with my life.

This is not an easy question to ask yourself, but you need to start somewhere. One thing was for sure—I did not want to continue with lab work. Shortly after beginning my master's, I realized that lab work was not my calling, and I needed to seriously consider other options.

My mother is a vice president at CanReg Inc., a regulatory consulting group, and this had landed me several summer jobs during college. The first summer I had the opportunity to work in quality services. The department was fairly new, and I got to take part in developing and rewriting standard operating procedures, as well as visiting clients who were undergoing ISO certification to help ensure they met the appropriate standards.

Quality services developed into a larger department with several full-time staff, and so I was moved into publishing and records. I spent the next two summers photocopying documents to be submitted to clients and government agencies worldwide. Through filing and managing the submissions library, I had the opportunity to touch all types of documents from clinical trial applications (CTAs) to adverse event reports (AERs) and medical device license applications. It gave me a sense of the depth of the healthcare products industry, but I still had no idea of what to expect when it came down to the work itself. I was able to see how people operated at the company—a lot of time was spent on the phone, in meetings with clients or writing documents, but I still was unsure of the knowledge that was required to be successful in the field.

Uncertain about the industry and hoping to blaze my own path in undiscovered territory, I considered my options. I held an honors degree in molecular biology and biotechnology from The University of Waterloo, and was completing my master's with a combined focus on molecular biology with biochemistry and plant physiology at The University of Western Ontario. I considered teaching, as I had loved being a teaching assistant, but with the poor job market during the recession, I was not sure where a teaching degree might land me. I wanted to give myself a name in an industry, and I wanted to do it soon. I was motivated to get somewhere and get going with my career, and I was not sure if teaching would enable that goal.

So what were my other options? Well, I had done a project for an undergraduate fermentation biology class concerning biological patents. Regulations, rules and law really interested me and I went above and beyond for that project. So, I considered pursuing patent law. But the prospect of law school was intimidating, and the courtroom seemed an unwelcoming place.

So what else was left? Regulatory. I had to ask myself the question: would I be riding on my mother's coattails? Would I be able to make my own name and blaze my own path while sharing the same name as an icon in the industry? Is this something that would actually interest me?

Regulatory affairs did seem the perfect fit—I enjoyed the ability to constantly learn and update my credentials. I valued the potential to climb the ladder and to become successful. Importantly, instead of being in the courtroom I would be writing or following the rules and regulations, and hopefully I would be able to affect them. I would be able to stay within the realm of science and up-to-date without completing lab work!

So, I looked into the regulatory options. I could take a course that would land me an internship, with luck leading to a full-time or contract position. Another option was to try to find a regulatory position. The latter seemed daunting, so I applied to the Humber Institute of Information and Technology's regulatory affairs program.

After applying, I was contacted by email and provided a time and location for an English comprehension and writing test. This was a little frightening. My undergraduate and master's degrees had not required any entrance tests. I went in not knowing what to expect, and was pleasantly surprised at how much I enjoyed it! The test was composed of English comprehension questions and a short essay. The comprehension questions were challenging but really sparked my curiosity because following the test I had to go home and look up the words I had not known.

The essay asked me to provide my opinion on something having to do with the healthcare industry. This seemed so general that I had a hard time trying to focus my thoughts. After a series of jot notes on what I thought the industry encompassed, I decided on my topic. I wrote about the Canadian drug approval system and its exceptionally stringent regulations that limited the products sent to Health Canada for approvals. I discussed why this could be a good thing—because it ensures the health and safety of Canadians—and why it could also pose a problem because it may stop certain drug companies from even submitting an application. I also discussed whether it would be worthwhile to even consider the Canadian market.

I thought I knew so much already.

Proud of my essay, I was fairly convinced I would get an interview. About a month later, I did receive an email instructing me to pick an interview time. I decided it was no time to be cocky, and I did a fair amount of research to ensure I would be prepared. Knowing I had some regulatory background, I was afraid I would be asked technical questions. So I went into the interview ready and very nervous, but I presented myself confidently. The interview was going well until I was notified that there were 450 applicants to the program for a mere 40 spots. Now my heart sank. This was the only option I had allowed myself for the September following my master's. I had not applied to any other programs, and I had no job prospects. I decided that I just had to be sure to charm these interviewers.

The interviewer, who was very upright and proper, asked about one of my publications for the Waterloo student newspaper, "Top 5 Scientific Pranks That Rocked the World." Although I tend to tailor my resumes to be professional and concise, I always like to include one interesting or entertaining point that the employer may read and remember me by, or prompt them to ask about during the interview. After I explained one of the specific pranks concerning an 18th century scientist from the University of Würzburg, the interviewer began laughing quite hysterically, and some very casual conversation followed until the interviewer realized he was about to miss the next appointment. This was a very good sign and I was quite pleased.

On the way out the door, the stern (yet still laughing) interviewer asked, "Now, you worked at CanReg Inc. And your last name is Anderson. Any relation to Patricia?" I could not avoid it! Even in my interview for this program I was being recognized. I realized it may not be such a bad thing and I smiled and admitted that I was her daughter.

Lo and behold, another month or so later I was notified that I was accepted into the program. After much celebration, I realized my regulatory experience could help me. Beginning classes I soon realized that the field was broader than

I could have ever imagined and the wealth of knowledge available to me even greater than expected.

Even after deciding on the regulatory field, I still had no clear-cut path to the type of job I wanted within the industry. Luckily there is a lot of mobility within the industry, because it may take some time to decide where to go.

Where could I possibly go? The government always seems to be a good idea because there is job security and you are part of the governing body, but a government position in Ottawa would take me away from my hometown near Toronto and my family. I could work in industry, but that opens up more questions: small start-up companies or big pharma? The small start-ups may provide unique opportunities, as you may be one of very few in the regulatory department, but the jobs may not be stable. The big pharmaceutical companies may have stable jobs, but may require you to fit into one niche area.

The considerations do not stop there. Once you have decided what type of place you would enjoy the most, you have to consider the sector—pharmaceuticals, biologics, natural health products, medical devices, agrichemicals, or even formularies and reimbursement.

So, I am still pursuing this regulatory affairs program and starting to get my name out in the field, but I have some advice. My suggestion to those beginning in the field is to look at your options early. Speak to people in the industry to see what may be a good fit for you. Join organizations such as the Regulatory Affairs Professionals Society (RAPS) and the Canadian Association of Professional Regulatory Affairs (CAPRA) to start networking and for avenues to start marketing yourself. Attend conferences and dinner meetings and volunteer. Do not be afraid to move within the industry or to try something new.

I am just excited to see where this industry can take me!

Chapter 22
How I Got Started in Regulatory

By Nancy Pire Smerkanich

Like most regulatory professionals, I never imagined that I would be doing what I do for a living. I especially did not imagine that I would still be doing it after 25 years in the industry. The path I followed was circuitous, but fun!

My story begins at the University of Connecticut where I received undergraduate degrees in both microbiology and Russian. The problem was, I hated bench work, which was really sad for a microbiology major, but I loved writing up labs and reports. I also wanted to go to medical school. But alas, in 1979, a microbiology and Russian major who had just returned from the former Soviet Union was not appealing to medical schools despite good grades and decent MCAT scores. With that path closed to me, I decided to attend graduate school and work in Boston. My first job out of college was at Children's Hospital Medical Center, where I was the research and medical school coordinator for the department of orthopedic surgery. Not long after I moved there, however, life intervened and I found myself getting married and moving to Philadelphia.

The primary industry in suburban Philadelphia was, and still is, pharmaceuticals. Merck was the main player, with its world headquarters located just a few miles from my home. I applied for a job and after more than a year and many interviews, I was hired as a biology quality control inspector. This entry-level job was meant primarily to groom folks to become biological manufacturing area managers. The problem was I hated manufacturing! I liked the process part and I loved the documentation aspects (auditing batch records), but I knew I was not cut out for managing the union staff. I was drawn to the regulatory aspects of the jobs I had held, which eventually led me to a position as a regulatory coordinator in the Merck Research Laboratories. I stayed in this position for seven years and learned more than I could have imagined. I worked in the cardio-renal area, which at the time was "the" place to be. I had the privilege of working with some wonderfully talented people and filed many Investigational New Drug applications (INDs) and New Drug Applications (NDAs). I was primarily US-focused and overall it was a great experience . . . until it was not.

Several things happened simultaneously that told me it was time to leave my position at Merck: my mentor left the company, my daycare center closed and my subscription to *Working Mother* magazine ran out. Perhaps the last item seems insignificant, but it was the final deciding factor. I decided the next stage in my career would be as a stay-at-home mother. Looking back now, I realize making this change was a very difficult decision, but I have never regretted it because it led me down a more significant path in my career.

I was at home for all of two weeks when I started getting calls to do part-time consulting work. This was very appealing as it allowed me to continue performing the regulatory work I enjoyed while giving me the flexibility to tend to my family. However, my husband maintained that I was still working full-time, just not getting paid for it. While I was doing regulatory consulting, I raised my two daughters and served as a Brownie troop leader, a Sunday School teacher, a homeroom mother, a member of the strategic planning committee for the school district and about 10 other things. Looking back, I have to agree this was perhaps more than a full-time schedule.

So, what started out as a two- or three-year hiatus from corporate life ended up lasting seven years. During this time, I made some wonderful regulatory discoveries and found out that a lot of what I thought of as "regulation" was actually "interpretation." I consider my time at big pharma to be the greatest learning experience of my life, but also realized that there is a lot one can learn on one's own and with small companies. There is in fact an infinite number of ways to get the job done or submit to the Food and Drug Administration (FDA)! During this time, I also learned that I loved to teach and train. But, most significantly, I learned the most important thing a regulatory professional can do—read. Read everything you can find that pertains to the subject at hand.

Two other significant events that occurred during my hiatus were the advent of the personal computer and the subsequent introduction of the Internet. Having such immediate access to a new world of regulatory subject matter dramatically changed my outlook on my career and the regulatory landscape. There was simply so much information to read! I soon realized that I needed to make a decision about what kind of regulatory work I wanted to pursue. I decided I needed to specialize because there was so much one person needed to know in order to be successful. My choices were to be a strategist in a particular therapeutic area or a generalist with either a US specific or global focus, or something more submissions related, which is where my interests are primarily focused. Whichever path I chose, it was clear that I better be good at using a computer!

As with many decisions in my life, I did not have to wait long for my next career step to present itself. I was often called in to help companies prepare their INDs and NDAs and I realized that I seemed to be good at this. In 1999, two things happened. First, the 1999 Electronic Submission Guidance was released by FDA, which allowed entire applications to be submitted electronically. Second, I was working at a company that was preparing, for the first time, an NDA with an electronic component. I felt that to prepare this application accurately, the electronic component needed to be consistent with the rest of the NDA. There were a few people in charge of this process and I found myself drawn to what they were doing and realized what an improvement these electronic submissions were over traditional paper submissions.

This was the beginning of the path that led me to my current job, where I am focused on electronic regulatory filings. This is an ideal job for me as it combines all the aspects of regulatory that I have always enjoyed. I have always loved the satisfaction of putting together filings, or as I used to tell my kids, the biggest research report you can imagine! I still love to teach and I am called on frequently to conduct public and private training for regulatory professionals. I get to work across all therapeutic areas, rather than focusing on a few. I also have the opportunity to interact regularly with FDA and I learn something new with every interaction. In fact, I am still learning. I attend and speak at many conferences, always looking to learn something new. Regulatory is an extremely dynamic area and it is not for the faint of heart or for people with low energy. To be successful, you have to want to evolve and you need to keep studying—regulations, guidances, information available via the *Freedom of Information Act Amendment* database and information on more websites than you could imagine.

I now lead a group of very smart and dedicated regulatory professionals. I travel all over the world as regulatory barriers are being challenged by a global economy. I teach courses at universities on subjects that were not available when I was in school and I still love what I do. I feel the most important aspect of my career is working on applications for drugs that have truly changed people's lives. Even though my role is not the "glamorous" one, and I have received no staggering moment of discovery or giant pat on the back from anyone, I know that I have contributed to treating disease and eradicating illness, which is an honor for any regulatory professional.

CHAPTER 23

How I Got Started in Regulatory

By Linda Bowen, MS, RAC

As a microbiology major graduating in the early 1980s, I faced slim opportunities for employment in my chosen career field. I searched for the "right job" for three months and, with no real prospects in sight, I decided to work for an upstart airline. I know, a far cry from regulatory affairs, but in the big picture, the 18 months I spent working there taught me a lot about myself and the business world.

I did eventually find my coveted microbiology position at a generic drug company in 1983. Fresh from the passage of the *Hatch-Waxman Act*, the generic drug business was growing. I was involved in all aspects of the three-person laboratory, from Quality Assurance to antibiotic development. And, oh yes, washing all the glassware!

I started to get the itch to find the "perfect job" about 18 months after joining the generic drug company. During a meeting of the local branch of the American Society of Microbiology, an acquaintance told me about an opportunity at a local, family-owned pharmaceutical company (note—networking, even among science nerds, does pay off). It was quality control microbiology work, but I would work closely with research and development at corporate headquarters; it was 10 miles from home and it meant a pay raise. I applied, interviewed and was hired. The year was 1985, and little did I know that I would spend the next 19 years working for this company and, eventually, the company that bought it, pursuing three different career paths.

Jump to 1988: I now had five years under my belt as a microbiologist and was burning out. I needed a change, but more importantly, I needed a challenge. Lab work just was not what I wanted to do. My boss saw that I was unhappy and suggested that I apply internally for one of the Quality Assurance (QA) positions that had been posted recently. It would mean a longer commute, as the position was at corporate headquarters, but this was my chance to move out of the lab. In the bigger picture, I realized if I were ever going to grow within the company, I would have to be where the action was.

QA was a welcome change and a challenge. I spent five years in QA. It was a great place to learn and interact with many different parts of the organization. I often had lunch with colleagues from other departments. One group, regulatory affairs, seemed to have a very exciting and highly visible presence. I tried to get the team to explain what they did, but they all seemed to struggle with a definition. One member of the group told me about a program she was attending at the Arnold & Marie Schwartz College of Pharmacy at Long Island University in pursuit of a master's degree in drug regulatory affairs. It was at night; I could commute with her and the company would pay for it. What was there to lose? So, in the autumn of 1992, I enrolled in the program. Within a few weeks, I began to understand why my lunchmates had difficulty defining their jobs. There was so much complexity and variety that it was hard to pinpoint—this was exciting stuff!

After the first semester, I was hooked! I continued in the program until 1993, when the unexpected happened; the person who had originally suggested that I attend the program decided to leave my company. But before she did, she told her boss that I would be a great replacement. He asked whether I would be interested in a position in the international regulatory affairs department. I do not remember saying yes, but I must have done so, as within the month, I started as a regulatory specialist.

And yes, I did receive my degree.

I had a great boss and mentor at that pharmaceutical company. He challenged me at every turn and kept me on my toes. By the time the company was sold in 2001, I had moved up the regulatory affairs ladder to associate director. I want to pay back the profession and can think of no better way than to mentor the next generation of regulatory professionals.

In summary:
- **Networking:** One of the most important tips I can give those breaking into the profession is to start networking. This need not be costly; it can be as simple as joining an online discussion or study group or a professional association that supports the regulatory function—the

Regulatory Affairs Professionals Society (RAPS), the Drug Information Association (DIA) or The Organisation for Professionals in Regulatory Affairs (TOPRA).

- **Mentoring:** perhaps your employer has a mentoring program. If you want to move up in the company or perhaps transition to a new area, look for a person you admire for passion and work ethic. Remember, mentoring is not the same as career counseling.
- **Communication skills:** These are important to a regulatory professional, whether for an internal meeting, a professional presentation or discussions with a health authority. I have found that volunteering to speak at internal meetings is a great way to prepare for the outside world. I honed my skills as a member of a community theatre, where I learned to become fearless in front of audiences. I also attended Toastmasters, a venue where my peers could assist and critique my style.
- **Volunteer:** Start a "lunch and learn" at your company or help with registration at local events—you need not be a presenter in order to become involved.
- **Challenge:** Accept challenge gracefully and let it be your driver. Be willing to learn, even if it is outside your comfort zone. You never know when it may come in handy. Do not be afraid to ask questions. We were all newcomers at one time!
- **Education:** There are many regulatory certificate, master's and doctorate programs available to you. This is a chance to learn, communicate and network.
- **"Hard knocks:"** Many of us started in the "school of hard knocks." You may need to work in a regulatory support function before getting the job you want.
- **Passion:** Have a passion for what you do; your job will be much easier and more enjoyable.

So here I am, 17 years after landing my first regulatory affairs position, and I have found that "perfect" career.

Chapter 24

How I Got Started in Regulatory

By Amy Grant

Once upon a time, I was a college student, majoring in English literature, working nights and weekends in Research Triangle Park (RTP), NC, at a research institute, conducting telephone surveys for the government. In addition, I had other temporary and part-time jobs teaching, tutoring, editing, proofreading and writing technical manuals with a focus on science and computers.

I kept hearing good things from colleagues about Burroughs Wellcome, an innovative company developing treatments for life-threatening diseases. I heard about their dedicated employees who had worked together for many years, particularly Gertrude Elion and George Hitchings, who won the Nobel Prize for their work on the treatment of disease and organ transplantation. Another employee, Bert Spilker, was championing orphan products and clinical innovation. I visited the company to pick up an application and diligently called the job hotline to check for openings that matched my qualifications. I applied for a documentation specialist position with the hope of having the security of one steady job, benefits and an opportunity for growth. This was also an opportunity to learn the biopharmaceutical business from the ground up.

I also applied for research and writing positions at other companies in RTP, but did not find the same sense of purpose, history and hope for the future that existed at Burroughs Wellcome. Some acquaintances who worked at the company had a certain light in their eyes as they talked about their work, the people at the company and the patients who would benefit from new medicines. The people at Burroughs Wellcome seemed to be working together on something greater than any one person. I wanted to be a part of such a creative and pioneering organization.

The interview process at Burroughs Wellcome was highly competitive, with both a panel interview and a computerized test on grammar, reading comprehension and writing. During the interview and the testing, I had a sense that my experience with science, love of languages and writing skills were a fit for the job. In addition, my experience volunteering for nonprofits and desire to contribute to the larger community seemed to fit the company's culture. It was important to me to find a workplace where people's actions spoke louder than words. And, I observed teamwork and dedication among company employees during my three-hour interview and previous visit to the reception area of the company. The company seemed to provide a balance of meaningful work and security for the future. This was very different than my series of part-time jobs since graduation, with a BA in English, and as a graduate student in English literature. I also remember laughing a lot during the interview and appreciating the interviewers' sense of humor.

At Burroughs Wellcome, the opportunity for continuous learning and exploration of science, computers and language was also extremely appealing. During my interview, it was exciting to see how the office design brought people together to work in clusters. Labs, documentation centers, research and development, legal, human resources and commercial departments were focused on specific work but were also connected. The company library was extraordinary, with smart librarians plus more tools and resources than any library I had ever encountered.

Best of all, Burroughs Wellcome was a big company acting like a small company. There seemed to be a culture of courtesy and respect when people greeted one another in the hallway. At the same time, it was obvious that employees had strong personalities and were very passionate about their work. So, I had a sense that conflict and debate came with the territory but with a common purpose.

I was hired at Burroughs Wellcome as a documentation specialist in the organizational development department, serving many departments, including regulatory. I worked in organizational development for about three years before transferring to the regulatory department. There were about 30 documentation specialists in organizational development, which created a supportive network with many opportunities for informal and formal training. Within two years, I had worked in most of the documentation centers and contributed to several major product development projects, approvals and launches. I had received several promotions as well as mentoring and support for continued education and personal development.

I enjoyed the work and received recognition for my editing, proofreading and writing skills. The company encouraged employees to contribute innovative ideas for improvement. I submitted several ideas and ended up chairing a cross-functional committee on workflow design. It was satisfying to see how research and discussion could have a positive impact on day-to-day work and the long-term success of product teams.

I worked on an electronic document management project and gained valuable regulatory experience by processing the components of Investigational New Drug applications (INDs), clinical trials exemptions (CTXs), New Drug Applications (NDAs), Marketing Authorisation Applications (MAAs) and other submissions. By the time I officially joined the regulatory department, I had detailed knowledge of cover letters, application forms, summaries, Investigator Brochures, clinical study reports, pregnancy registries, case report forms, tabulations, datasets, etc. My position in the organizational development department also provided the opportunity for networking across the company and for on-the-job training in my job or in other areas I was interested in.

Eventually, after Glaxo purchased Burroughs Wellcome, I transferred to the electronic publishing group in regulatory operations and had the opportunity for in-depth cross-training in other regulatory areas. The senior regulatory team provided a basic training program and encouraged staff to learn and apply what we learned to our current and future work. Seasoned regulatory professionals were eager to share their knowledge and experience—a great way to start in regulatory.

Glaxo's culture was very different from Burroughs Wellcome's, but was consistent in the opportunities for continuous learning and growth. When I look back, I realize that it is true that perspective and timing are everything. Since we spend so much time at work, it is important to surround ourselves with as many helpful people as possible. In the end, we have choices, no matter how difficult a situation may seem. I believe we get out of life what we put into it and what goes around comes around. I learned the most from difficult people, challenging situations and bad choices that I made along the way.

My solid foundation in regulatory has sustained me throughout the years and has given me the courage to explore many regulatory areas including management, regulatory operations, chemistry, manufacturing and controls (CMC) and policy and intelligence. It has been fascinating to consider the whole puzzle instead of only focusing on the pieces. One of my favorite parts of the job has been to help others help themselves, including working with student interns. It is a gift to see things go full circle and to be able to pass along the passion for helping patients and workplace survival skills so generously shared by others. Despite many difficult situations, every day in regulatory affairs is a chance to make difference.

INDEX

A
Abbreviated New Drug Application (ANDA), 88–89
Affymax, 147
American Medical Writers Association (AMWA), 141
Anderson, Stephanie, 155–158
Association of American Medical Schools (AAMS), 150
Association of Records Managers and Administrators (ARMA), 24

B
Bioequivalence, 88–89
Biological License Application (BLA), 135
Biotechnology Industry Organization (BIO), 9
Bowen, Linda, 163–165
Brown-Tuttle, Meredith, 153–154
Burroughs Wellcome, 167–169
Business development, 40–43

C
California Separation Science Society, 22
Canadian Association of Professional Regulatory Affairs (CAPRA), 22, 158
CanReg, Inc., 155–157
Center for Professional Innovation & Education (CfPIE), 15
Certification, 8, 13–14, 36, 90, 117, 151–152
Chemistry, manufacturing and controls (CMC), 85, 93
    career specialization, 81, 95–101
    section development & review process, 97–99
    training requirements, 100–101
Client relationship development, 35–36, 39, 41–43, 45, 50
Clinical research
    graduate coursework in, 150, 154
    personal professional experience in, 153–154
    professional scope and responsibilities, 81, 83–84, 113–117
Code of Federal Regulations, Part 21, 137
Common Technical Document (CTD)
    overview, 122–123, 135–137
    regulatory writing of, 133–135, 139
Communication
    challenges, 27–29
    large pharmaceutical regulatory requirements, 62–67
    role in independent consulting, 31, 34
    role in regulatory writing, 142–143
    skill required in regulatory, 3, 128, 151–152, 161, 165
    small pharmaceutical regulatory requirements, 69, 81
Conferences, 22–23
Confidential disclosure agreement (CDA), 49
Conroy, Christine, 145–147
Contract research organization (CRO), 54, 115–116, 151
Contracts, 49
Cook Medical, 150–151
Cranfield University, 17, 20–21

D
Declaration of Helsinki, 138
Direct-to-Consumer (DTC), 108
Division of Drug, Marketing, Advertising and Communications (DDMAC), 104–105, 146
Document management, 124–125, 168–169
Document management systems (DMS), 120, 125
Drug development, 134–135
Drug Information Association (DIA), 8–10, 22, 24, 141, 165
    conferences, 23
    Special Interest Area Community—Regulatory Intelligence Group, 127
Drug Price Competition and Patent Term Restoration Act of 1984 (Hatch-Waxman Act), 89
Due diligence, 131
Dynamic equlibrium, 26–27

E
Education
    RA certification and certificate programs, 13–18
    RA master's and doctoral programs, 18–22
electronic Common Technical Document (eCTD)
    conferences and training, 23–24
    regulatory requirements, 123–124
Electronic submissions
    eCTD filing requirements, 123–124
    FDA standards, 124
    regulatory writer role in, 139–140

INDEX

systems support role in, 119–120
Emergo Group, 151–152
European Federation of Pharmaceutical Industries and Associations (EFPIA), 9
European Medicines Agency (EMA), 123

F
Food and Drug Administration (FDA)
   advertising and promotion oversight, 103–104, 108–109
   CTD & eCTD requirements, 122–123
   Office of Generic Drugs, 89
Food and Drug Law Institute (FDLI), 151

G
Gap analysis, 32
Generic drug company
   advancement potential, 91–93
   drug development & approval overview, 87–89
   organizational structure, 89–90
   personal professional experience in, 163
   position and level assessment, 89–91
   regulatory skills required in, 90–91
Generic drugs, 87–89
Genitope, 146–147
GlaxoSmithKline, 169
Government contractor, 114–115
Grant, Amy, 167–170

H
Health Insurance Portability and Accountability Act (HIPAA), 138
Health Level Seven (HL7) Standards, 124
Hoffmann-LaRoche, 146
Hood College, 15
Human dynamics, 25–30
Humber Institute of Information and Technology, 156–157

I
Image Solutions, Inc., 23
Independent consultant
   career strategy, 33–34
   definition, 31
   skills required, 34–43, 45–51
   typical projects, 31–33
Information technology (IT) systems
   independent consultant requirements, 38, 48–49
   large pharmaceutical company requirements, 62
   systems support specialist role in, 120
   XML technology, 123
Institute of Validation Technology (IVT), 23
Institutional Review Board (IRB), 116–117, 135
International Conference on Harmonisation (ICH), 122, 133–134, 137–138
International Federation of Pharmaceutical Manufacturers and Associations (IFPMA), 9
International Society for Pharmaceutical Engineering (ISPE), 9
Investigational New Drug (IND) applications
   filing of, 115
   regulatory writing and, 134–135

J
Johns Hopkins University, 18

K
Keck Graduate Institute of Applied Life Sciences, 18–19

L
Laws, interpretation, 26–27
Lehigh University, 15–16
Loh, Evangeline D., 149–152
Long Island University - Arnold and Marie Schwartz College of Pharmacy, 19, 164

M
Maslow, AH, 26
Massachusetts College of Pharmacy, 19
Mentors, 81, 140–141, 165, 169
Merck, 159–160
Mills, CW, 25
Money management, 37–38, 47–48

N
National Cancer Institute (NCI), 114
National Institutes of Health Division of AIDS, 115
Networking
   finding mentors, 81, 140–141, 165, 169
   independent consulting, 31, 36, 45–46
   large pharmaceutical companies and, 66–67
   support group and organization involvement,

INDEX

9–10, 164–165 (*See also* Volunteering)
New Drug Application (NDA), 95–96, 135
Nonclinical safety, 81, 83
North Carolina Regulatory Affairs Forum (NCRAF), 9–10
Northeastern University College of Professional Studies
  certificate programs, 16
  master of science degree programs, 19, 21

O
O'Connor and McDermott, 25–26
Organizations, regulatory, 7–10

P
Parenteral Drug Association (PDA), 9–10, 22
Pharmaceutical companies, large
  myths associated with RA employment, 61–62
  organizational structure, 54–57
  personal professional experience in, 159–160, 168–169
  product lifecycle management, 55–56
  RA careers in, 53–54, 57–59, 61
  skills required for regulatory, 63–67
Pharmaceutical companies, small
  advancement potential, 74–75, 84–86
  organizational structure, 69–70, 79–80
  position and level assessment, 80–81, 83–84
  pros and cons, 77, 158
  skills required for regulatory, 69–73, 80
  transitioning from large pharma company, 73–74, 147
Pharmaceutical Education Research Institute (PERI), 141
Pharmaceutical Research and Manufacturers of America (PhRMA), 9
Pharmaceutical Sciences Group, 22
Prescription Drug User Fee Act (PDUFA), 122
Product Quality Lifecycle Implementation (PQLI), 9
Project management, 32–33, 91
Project Management Institute (PMI), 24
Promotional regulatory
  professional responsibilities, 104, 107–108, 110–111
  scope, 103–104
Promotional review board/medical, legal and regulatory team (PRB/MLR), 104–106
PTi International, 23
Publishing, regulatory, 120–122, 155–156
Purdue University
  graduate certificate program, 17
  master of science degree programs, 19

Q
Quality assurance/Quality control, 81, 83, 155, 159–160, 163–164

R
Reference listed drug (RLD), 87–88
Regulations, interpretation, 26–27
Regulator Affairs Certification (RAC), 8, 36, 90, 117, 151–152
Regulatory
  career paths, 1–2, 81, 83–84, 113
  degree discrimination, 71, 73
  human dynamics affecting process, 25–30
  independent consulting, 31–42, 160–162
  large pharmaceutical company employment in, 53–59, 61–67
  multidisciplinary profession, 8
  training role in, 161
  transitioning into, 76, 145–147
Regulatory affairs
  certification & certificate programs, 13–18
  master's & doctoral programs, 18–22
  personal professional experience in, 149–152
  scope, 13
  typical projects, 31–32
Regulatory Affairs Professionals Society (RAPS), 8–10, 22, 24, 36, 113, 117, 141, 158, 165
  certification, 8, 13–14. 152
  conferences, 23
  Online University RA certificate programs, 14–15
Regulatory intelligence
  definition and scope, 127–129
  primary functions of, 129–131
  skills required in, 38, 128–129
Regulatory operations
  certification and training, 23–24, 126
  document management function, 124–125
  personal professional experience in, 155–156, 168–169
  publisher function, 120–122

173

INDEX

scope, 22–23, 119
skills required in, 125–126
systems support function, 119–120
Regulatory Scope of Practice and Compensation Report, 8
Regulatory writer
  education and training, 141–142
  scope of work, 133–134
  skills required, 137–140, 142–143

S

San Diego State University
  certificate program, 15
  master of science degree program, 21
Seneca College of Applied Arts and Technology, 15
Senge, Peter, 29–30
Skills
  analytical, 29–30, 70, 128
  business, 38–40, 140
  communication, 3, 27–31, 34, 62–67, 128, 142–143, 151–152, 161, 165
  detail oriented, 35, 126
  flexibility, 27, 31, 46, 67, 73, 126
  negotiation, 30, 34–35, 70, 128
  networking, 10, 30, 33–34, 46, 64, 66–67, 70, 81, 110–111, 128, 158, 163–164
  scientific and technical knowledge, 63–64, 90–91, 138–139, 161
  self-motivation, 34, 46
  surveillance, 130–131
  time management, 34, 46
  writing, 63, 69, 140
Smerkanich, Nancy Pire, 159–162
Social & Scientific Systems, Inc. (SSS), 114–116
Social media, 108–110
Socialized power, 28–29
Special Libraries Association (SLA), 9–10
Specialization
  CMC, 81, 95–101
  regulatory, 2, 54, 81, 83–84, 90–91
St. Cloud State University, 19
Support groups, regulatory, 7–10
Syntex Laboratories, Inc., 145–146

T

Temple University
  pre- and post-master's certificates programs, 16–17
  School of Pharmacy masters degree programs, 19–20
The Organisation for Professionals in Regulatory Affairs (TOPRA), 8–10, 22, 165
  master of science degree programs, 20
  postgraduate certificate program, 17
Thomson Reuters (Liquent), 23

U

University of Georgia College of Pharmacy
  certificate program, 18
  master of science degree program, 20
University of Southern California
  master of science degree program, 21
  Ph.D program, 21–22
University of Washington Extension, 15

V

Volunteering, 3–5, 9–10, 165. *See also* Networking

W

Webinars, 22–23
Writing. *See* Regulatory writer

X

XML technology, 123, 139–140

Acronyms Used in this Book

A
ANDA
Abbreviated New Drug Application (US)

B
BLA
Biologics License Application (US)

C
CAPRA
Canadian Association of Professional Regulatory Affairs

CGMP
Current Good Manufacturing Practice

CMC
Chemistry, Manufacturing and Controls

CRO
Contract research organization

CTA
Clinical Trial Application

CTD
Common Technical Document

D
DDMAC
Division of Drug Marketing, Advertising, and Communications (US Food and Drug Administration)

DIA
Drug Information Association

DTC
Direct-to-consumer

E
eCTD
Electronic Common Technical Document

EMA
European Medicines Agency

Acronyms Used in this Book

F
FDA
US Food and Drug Administration

G
GCP
Good Clinical Practice

GMP
Good Manufacturing Practice

GxP
Good Pharmaceutical Practices

I
ICH
International Conference on Harmonisation of Technical Requirements for Registration of Pharmaceuticals for Human Use

IDE
Investigational Device Exemption

IND
Investigational New Drug Application

IRB
Institutional Review Board

M
MAA
Marketing Authorization Application

N
NB
NDA
New Drug Application (US)

P
PhRMA
Pharmaceutical Research and Manufacturers Association

PMA
Premarket Approval Application

Acronyms Used in this Book

Q
QA
Quality Assurance

QC
Quality Control

R
RA
Regulatory Affairs

RAC
Regulatory Affairs Certification

RAPS
Regulatory Affairs Professionals Society

RLD
Reference Listed Drug

RO
Regulatory Operations

S
SEC
Securities and Exchange Commission

SOP
Standard operating procedure

T
TOPRA
The Organisation for Professionals in Regulatory Affairs

X
XML
Extensible Markup Language